Robot Design Techniques
MANGA TECHNIQUES
Vol.3

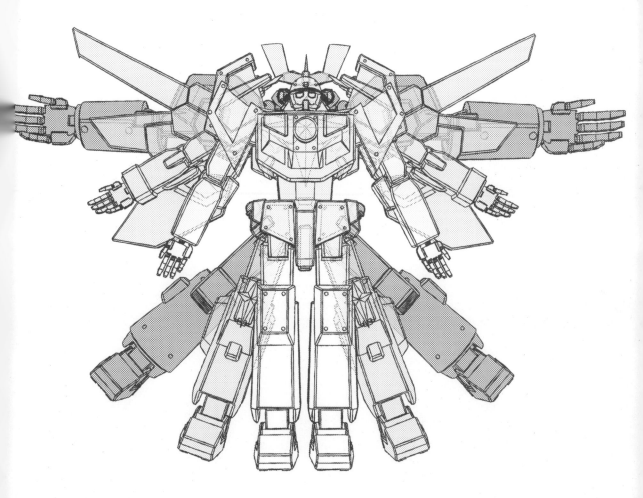

An Instruction Manual for Manga Artists Around the World

MANGA TECHNIQUES Vol.3
Robot Design Techniques for Beginners

Copyright © 2002 S.E.Inc

First published in 2002 by S.E.Inc.
1-20-60 Miyauchi, Nakahara-ku, Kawasaki City 211-0051, Japan

Editing:Shunji Haraguchi
Cover art and Composition:Yamano Takashi

All rights reserved.No part of this publication may be reproduced,
stored in a retrieval system, or transmitted in any form or by any means,
electronic, mechanical, photocopying, recording or otherwise,
without the prior written permission of the publisher.

Distributor
Japan Publications Trading Co,Ltd.
1-2-1 Sarugaku-cho, Chiyoda-ku,Tokyo 101-0064,Japan
E-mail:jpt@jptco.co.jp
URL:http://www.jptco.co.jp/

First printing: December 2002
Second printing:January 2003

ISBN 4-88996-099-6
Printed in Japan

CONTENTS

Chapter 1 Before You Begin Drawing — 05

Boy-shaped Robot	06
Girl-shaped Robot	07
How to Create Three Dimensional Drawing with Perspectives	09
Silhouette determines the feeling of the robot	12
Basics for Drawing Parts for Human-shaped Robot	13

Chapter 2 The Head — 15

Basics for Drawing the Head with Perspectives	16
Different Ways to Draw the Eyes (Camera)	18
Different Ways to Draw the Nose, Mouth, etc.	20
Different Ways to Draw the Neck	22
Different Ways to Draw the Head/with Perspectives	24
Samples of Frames Using the Head	26

Chapter 3 The Body — 27

Basics for Drawing the Body with Perspectives	28
Different Ways to Draw the Chest (Straight lines)	30
Different Ways to Draw the Chest (Curved lines)	32
Different Ways to Draw the Hip	34
Optional Equipments for the Back/How to Attach Them	36
Different Ways to Draw the Body with Perspectives	38
Samples of Frames Using the Body	40

Chapter 4 The Arms — 41

Basics for Drawing the Arms	42
Different Ways to Draw the Elbow Joints/Human-shaped Arms	44
Different Ways to Draw the Hands/Palms	46
Different Ways to Draw Nonhuman-like Arms	48
Different Ways to Draw Handheld Weapons	50
Different Ways to Draw the Arms with Perspectives	52
Samples of Frames Using the Arms	54

Chapter 5 The Legs — 55

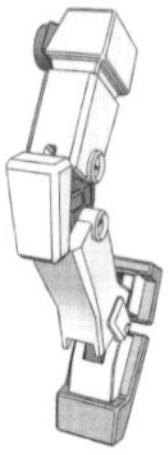

Basics for Drawing the Legs	56
Different Ways to Draw Human-shaped Legs and Knees	58
Different Ways to Draw Nonhuman-like Legs	60
Different Ways to Draw Parts Below the Ankles	62
Different Ways to Draw the Legs with Perspectives	64
Samples of Frames Using the Legs	66

Chapter 6 Variety of Robot Design — 68

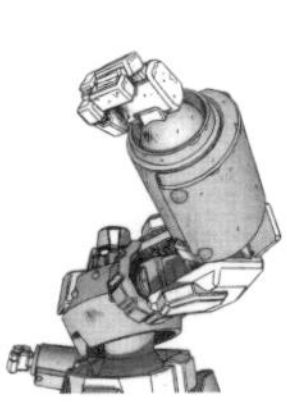

Variety of Robot Design	69
Hero Mechanical Robot (Slender Type)	70
Massive Robot	72
Monster Robot	74
Female Robot (Adult)	76
Female Robot (Young)	78
Multi-legged Robot	80

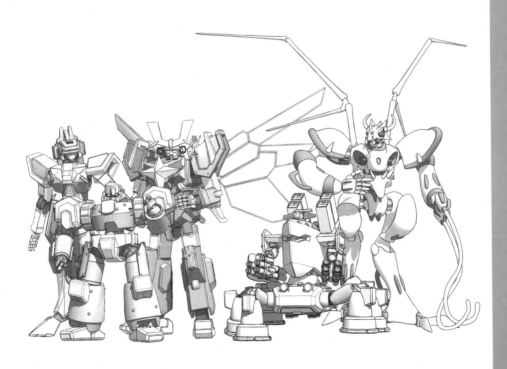

CHAPTER 1
Before You Begin Drawing

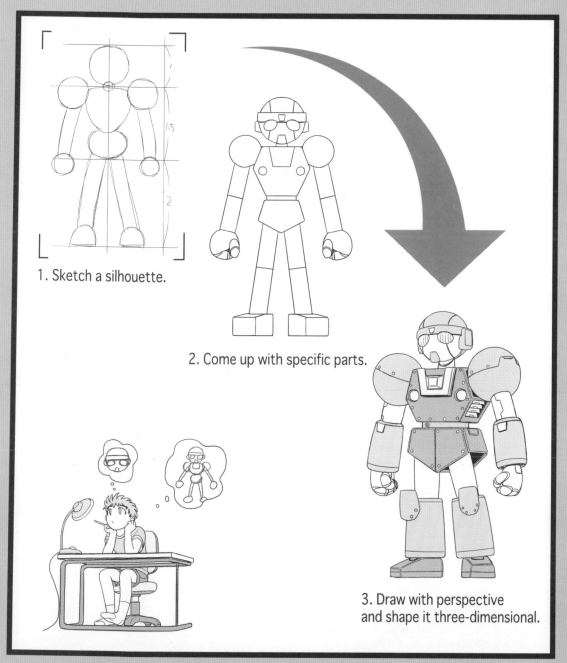

1. Sketch a silhouette.
2. Come up with specific parts.
3. Draw with perspective and shape it three-dimensional.

Before you start, you should know the basics of drawing a robot. In this chapter, you will draw a boy (girl) robot by drawing a rough silhouette, then coming up with the parts, and finally using perspective.

Boy-shaped Robot

The directions for drawing a robot for the first time.

Before doing anything, put the ideas together. Draw a boy-shaped robot this time. He will be standing and facing forward.

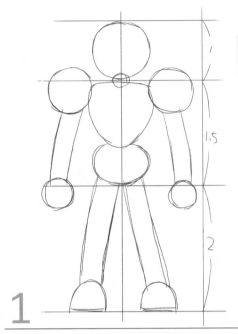

1 Use the pencil and come up with a well-balanced silhouette. It will be much easier if you draw a few base lines. The balance is up to you, but for the moment it is 1:1.5:2 from the head, body to legs.

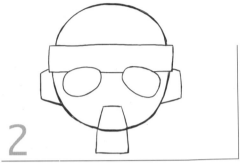

2 First, draw the head. Use circles throughout, making the eyes almond-shaped, except for the mouth, which we will shape with a square. Make the top look like a helmet.

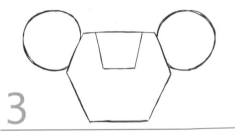

3 Now, we will draw the chest. Draw a hexagon with the top a little wider, and then draw a square under where the neck will be placed. Draw circle-shaped shoulders so they will look strong.

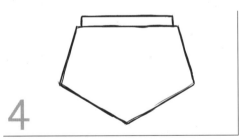

4 Now the hip. Draw a pentagon to make it seem like he is wearing a pair of shorts. Draw the waist a little thinner than the hip.

5 Draw the arms and legs. Draw them straight to create a slender look. Put a parallel line on each joint.

Girl-shaped Robot

Now it is time to draw a girl-shaped robot.

Put your thoughts together. This time, she will have pigtails down her shoulders and will be wearing a skirt. She will be standing and facing forward.

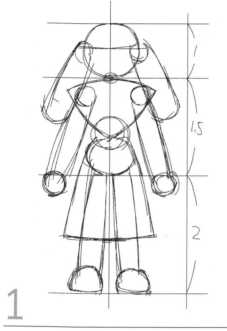

1

First, use the pencil and come up with a well-balanced silhouette. Then add the pigtails and the skirt. Same as the boy robot, the balance will be 1:1.5:2 from the head, body to legs.

2

Draw the head. Use circles primarily except for the mouth. Make the mouth smaller than the boy's. Add bangs and pigtails.

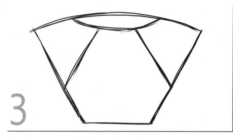

3

Next, we will draw the chest. Draw a rectangle wide at the top and draw in a line under where the head will be. Put two extra lines along the shoulders to make them seem like they can move.

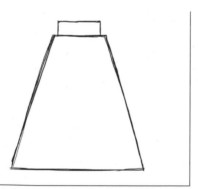

4

Now, draw the hip. Draw a skirt with the bottom flared. Draw the waist by adding a couple more lines on the top of the skirt.

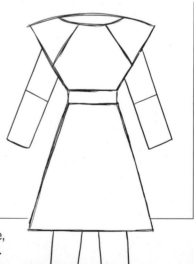

5

Draw the arms and legs. Draw them with straight lines as before, but this time a little narrower. Put in a line each along the joints.

Boy-shaped Robot

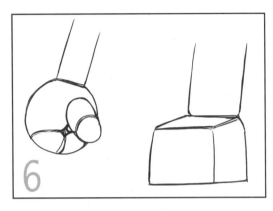

6

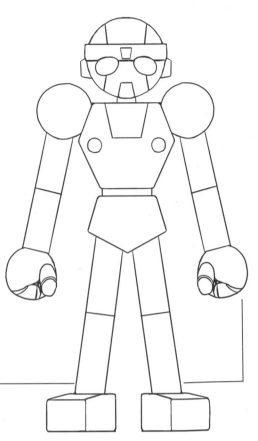

Draw the hands and feet. Use circles for the hands and fingers, but rectangles for the feet. Draw them larger than the arms and legs to generate a feeling of strength and power.

7

Finally, draw in all the meters and devices on the head and chest. We are finished.

Girl-shaped Robot

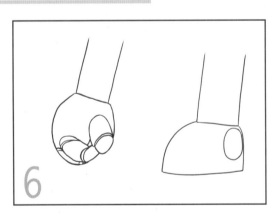

6

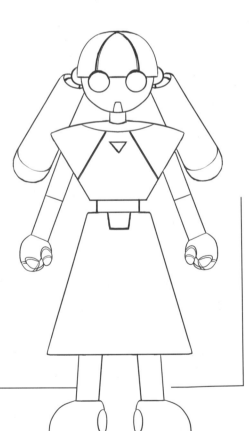

Draw the hands and feet. Use circles for the hands and fingers, but rectangles for the feet. To generate softness, draw them rounder than those of the boy's.

7

Add a little more detail and we are done.

How to Create Three Dimensional Drawing with Perspective

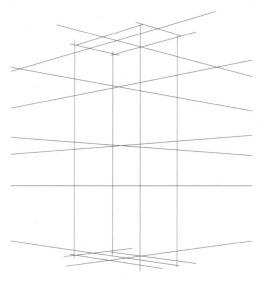

The drawing should be drawn from a side angle. It is ideal if the drawing only contained rectangular shapes, however, that is not always the case. When drawing with round shapes, draw by trying to see past through the shapes.

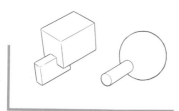

Your drawings will improve greatly when you become able to draw three-dimensional objects precisely.

Change the thickness of the joints.

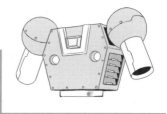

When you are able to design the robots with right perspective, try to add in details like nails and joints.

A little different from before when the robots were facing forward, these designs are much more realistic.

We have drawn both the boy and girl-shaped robots three dimensionally.

By adding depth to the illustration, it now looks improved and with more information.

Drawing the robots facing forward can sometimes make them look dull and flat. Thus, it is better, most of the times, to draw them in an angle to show the audience what the robots truly look like.

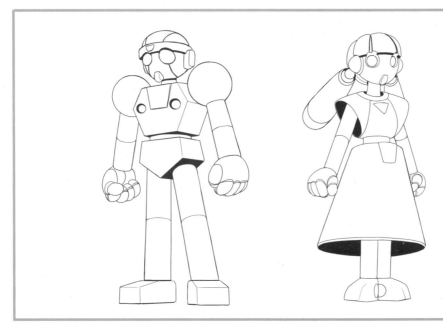

When you draw three dimensionally, the point of focus and the vanishing point become very important.
These robots here are drawn with the focus on their ankles and with an upward angle to make the robots seem big. (The latter technique is used to film plastic models.)

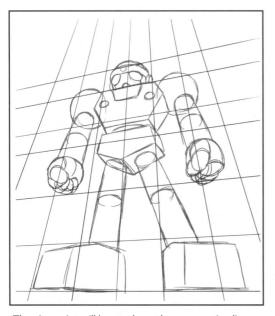

The best way to make a robot seem gigantic is to draw it with an upward angle and with perspective. With perspective, things near the focus will seem large when things far from the focus will seem small. Although drawing using the vanishing point enables you to draw precisely, you should be able to draw with perspective without using the point after you've gotten used to this technique. Keep in mind that with an upward angle, the feet and legs of a massive robot should seem larger compared to the other parts of the body. Use this technique effectively.

However, this technique cannot be very effective when drawing robots with thin arms and legs.
The limbs may seem short due to the perspective.
In this case, draw the limbs a little larger than usual or use the perspective in another way to avoid it.

The viewpoint will be at where the perspective lines are parallel.

Practice Drawing with Perspective

We will practice using rectangular solids to show the effects of adding the right perspective.

Draw a rectangular solid using two-point perspective.

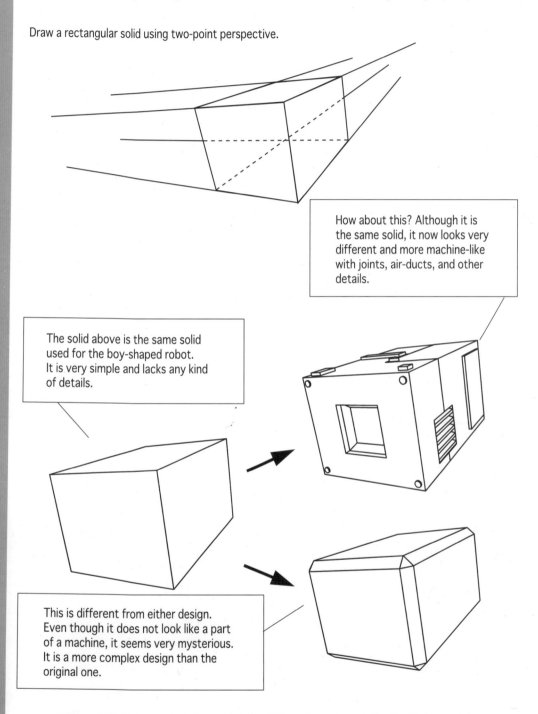

How about this? Although it is the same solid, it now looks very different and more machine-like with joints, air-ducts, and other details.

The solid above is the same solid used for the boy-shaped robot. It is very simple and lacks any kind of details.

This is different from either design. Even though it does not look like a part of a machine, it seems very mysterious. It is a more complex design than the original one.

These two different techniques, called the adding of density and detail addition, can become very useful when designing robots. Robot designs without much detail can be very dull, especially at scenes when the robots are focused up and close. Robots with flat surface and simple body and limbs can benefit from these techniques. But, at the same time, remember that adding too much detail can make the robots just chunks of complicated lines.

Silhouette determines the feeling of the robot.

The silhouettes are copies of the same robot with different parts of its body magnified or shrunk.

This is the original silhouette of the robot. Its small head and long legs double its image of a huge robot. Also the broad chest and the extended shoulder covers show its strength.

We have shrunk both its arms and legs, and the shape resembles a penguin. The limbs are now incapable of carrying out their original task, but the arms can be used as weapons, and the legs can be replaced with tires or wheels. The legs might be folded and can be extended upon use. The unusual figure gives a mysterious feeling to the robot.

The accent is on its arms. The gorilla-like silhouette makes its arms seem very strong.

This one has the emphasis on the legs. Like an ostrich, its legs are unusually long, and the arms seem too short to be of any use. However the arms might be some kind of weapons. Because of the legs, the robot seems capable of running very fast, but the legs generate a clumsy image.

This time we have slightly thinned down the tips of its limbs. The thinning down makes the robot seem more human-like and light. Because of these effects, which go against the usual images of robots - usually strong and masculine, this silhouette is hardly used.

Powerful Type. We have made each detail wider, especially the tip of its elbows and knees, to bring out masculinity.

The silhouette is modified to bring out speediness. Less width and longer legs make the robot seem swift.

We have added a few weapons for this one. The weapons give an upgraded effect on the robot. The advantage of this type is that you can vary the weapons. It is also possible to replace the weapon with something else.

Now the accent is on its head. Because of its head, it has a child-like figure. This kind is often used as ally/friend robots, but sometimes they are used as giants. In the latter case, the head usually has a special function with weapons inside it.

This time we have added some extra parts. By adding wings, the silhouette changes dramatically. The horns on its head give originality and superiority to the robot.

Basics for Drawing Parts for Human-shaped Robot and Shortcuts

The Head - P15

Compared to other parts, the head can have the most human-like qualities. However, it is also possible to design a robot without its head.

The Body - P27

It is an essential part bringing the head, arms and legs together. The large surface area calls for attention to details and accents.

Nonhuman-like Arms - P48

It is possible to replace the arms with weapons.

The Legs - P55

Legs are the means of transportation for the robot. Legs are essential if designing a human-shaped robot, however, you can also design a robot lacking its legs.

The Arms - P41

Arms can be used to grab, attack and use tools and weapons. You can make a tank look like a robot just by adding arms to it.

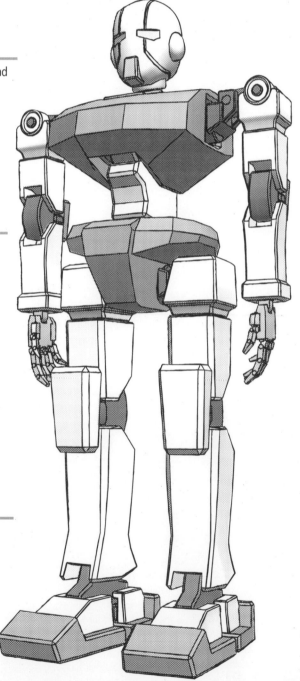

The back of a robot can be easily forgotten. However, it is very important to put in as much detail as you can for the other parts of the body.

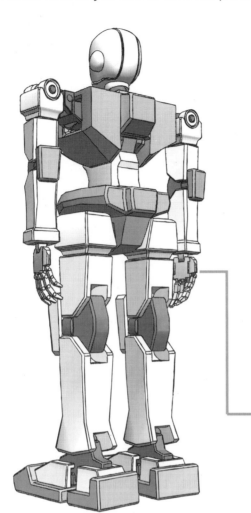

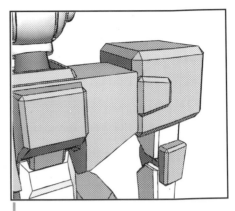

Shoulder covers

Designs with shoulder covers are very popular. We will talk about them on the body parts corner.

Most of the times, the middle part only serves as a joint.

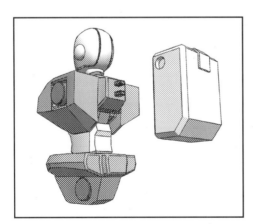

Optional Parts for the Back - P37

Designs for backpacks and related tools for the robots. They are usually exchangeable.

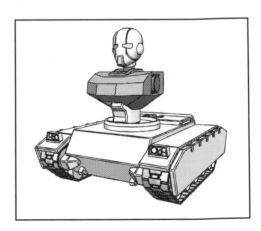

Nonhuman-like Legs - P58

The lower part can be replaced with crawlers and/or wheels.

The part under the hip is usually considered the lower part of the robot.

CHAPTER 2
The Head

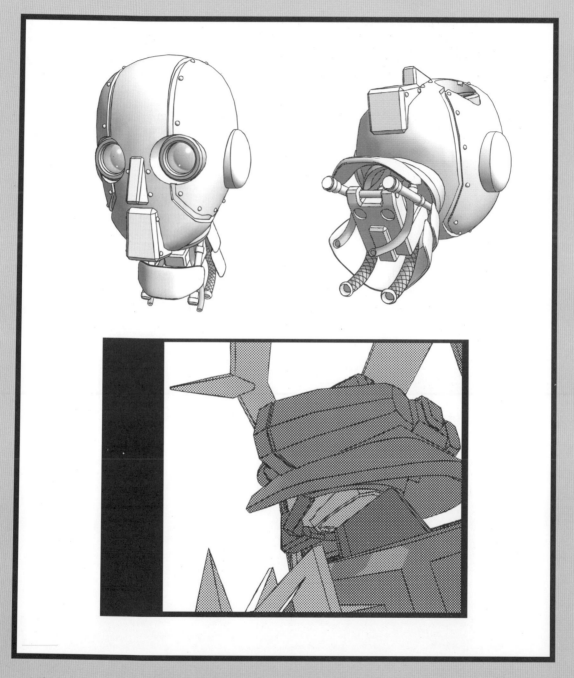

Like drawing a human being, remember that it is possible to change the expressions on the robots' faces. The eyes act as cameras. There are ways to draw the head other than human-shaped.

Basics for Drawing the Head with Perspectives

We used the human head to design the fundamental shape.

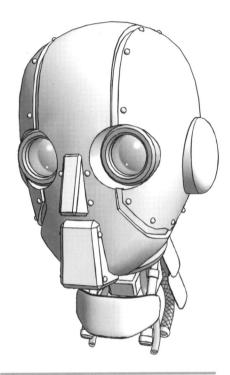

Front perspective

<Pointers>

■ Different ways to draw the eyes
(They are the most important parts.)

■ Different ways to draw the nose and mouth
(They can be designed together as one.)

■ Different ways to draw the neck
(Keep in mind that the neck connects the head and the chest.)

■ Different ways to draw nonhuman-like head

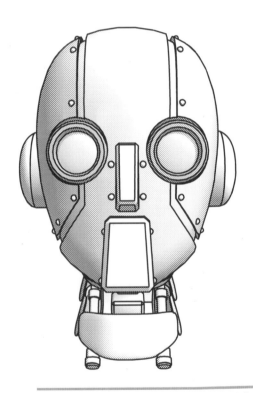

Facing forward

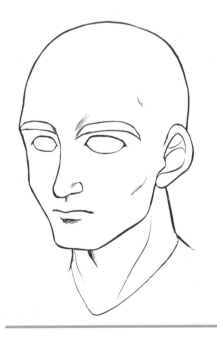

Use a diagonal angle to design the silhouette. Keep in mind the perspective while drawing.

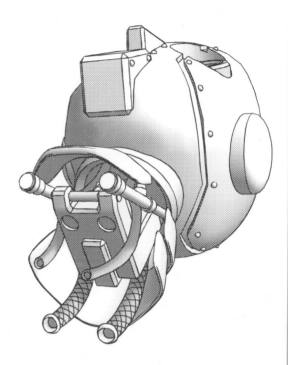

Upward perspective

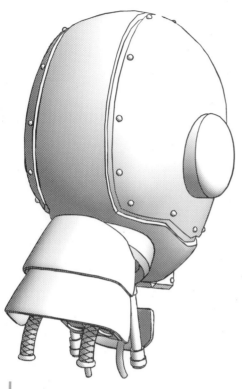

Back perspective

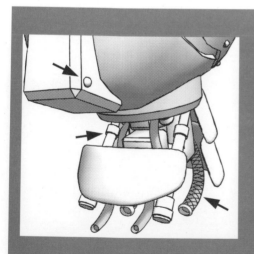

You can make the design more realistic by adding cylinders, tubes and other mechanical parts on the joint of the neck.

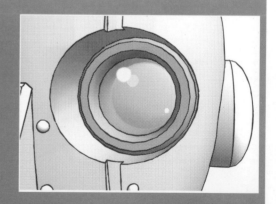

Draw a lens inside the eye. By putting in some highlights, the robot becomes more realistic and lively.

Different Ways to Draw the Eyes (Camera)

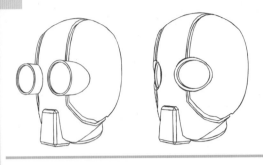

Round Eyes
The roundness of the eye creates a silly atmosphere.
Projected and Dented
(Different expressions using the same shape)

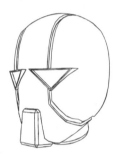 

Polygonal Eyes
This shape is often used for hero robots.

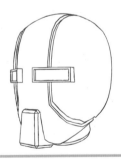 

Triangle Eyes
By giving them some angles, the face becomes more lively.

Square Eyes
The square shape gives a calm and cool feeling to the face.

Almond-shaped Eyes
This shape gives a human quality to the face.

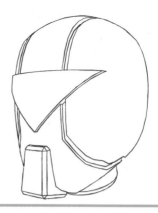

Goggle-shaped Eyes
It can be used to bring out seriousness.

Masked Eyes
This shape is often used for heroes.

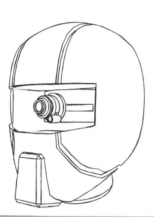

Mono-eye
This design is useful to create strangeness/oddness.

Camera Type
Suitable for machines.

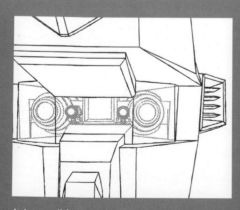
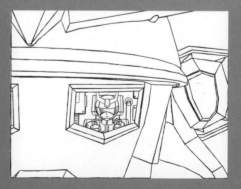

It is possible to make the cameras seem more machine-like with the way you draw in details on the lenses and censor.

The eyes need not be cameras, and can be cockpits, which are popular for hero robots.

Different Ways to Draw the Nose, Mouth, etc.

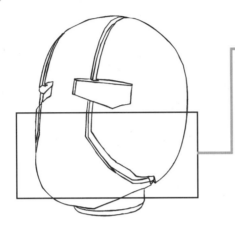

This part is frequently ignored, however, it comes in handy when creating many robots and trying to put character and originality in each one.

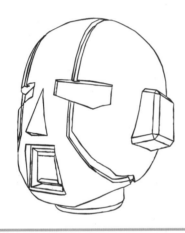

A human-like triangle nose, a dented and square mouth, and three-dimensional ears.

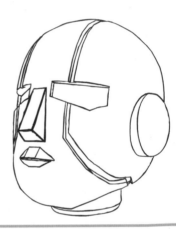

A human-like square nose, a human-like mouth with lips, and round ears.

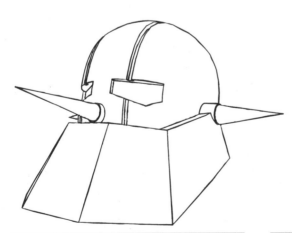

A cone nose, a beard-like mouth, and cone ears.

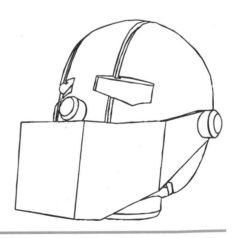

A button-shaped nose, a square mouth that can be opened or closed, and button-shaped ears.

Just by combining different parts together, you can make a variety of faces fit for any kind of jobs, and also add personality to each robot.

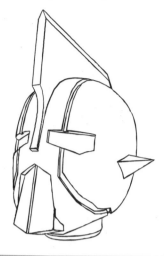

A nose connected to a crest, a vertical mouth, and pyramid ears.

A long vertical nose and slit-shaped ears.

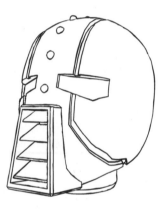

A nail-shaped nose and a duct-shaped mouth.

A masked mouth and duct-shaped ears.

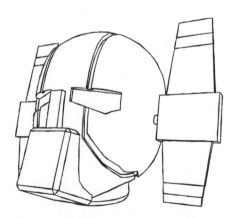

A cube-shaped nose and mouth, and antennae ears.

Different Ways to Draw the Neck

This part can become hidden depending on the design, but it is very close to the head and nevertheless important. These examples can be used for joints of the other parts of the body.

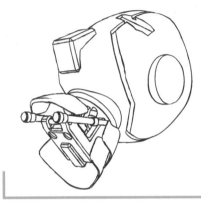

Armor Type
This type is very common in hero robots. Strong-looking, fewer lines.

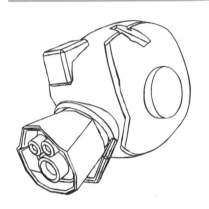

Oil Pressure Cylinders Type
This design is often seen in designs for realistically looking robots. However, it involves many lines.

Magnetic Joint Type
Although this design is not so common, it is an attractive piece and very easy to get nice scenes out of it. Only few lines are needed.

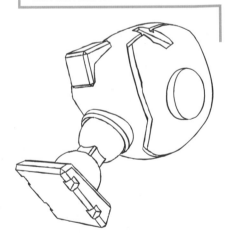

Motor Type
This design is commonly seen in realistically looking robots.
This design requires only few lines.

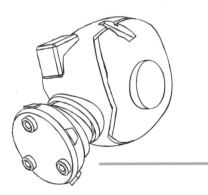

Ring Cover Type
Even though this design is not so common, it looks very strong. The rings resemble the joints on the clothing used for deep-sea operations.

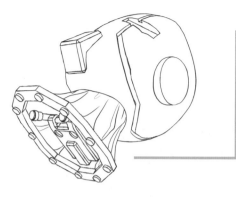

Cloth-covered Type
It is often used for realistically looking robots. It is actually used in real life robots. Remember that the machineries are beneath the cover.

Hover Type
Although uncommon, this design can be used for robots made with advanced/outer space science. Very easily drawn.

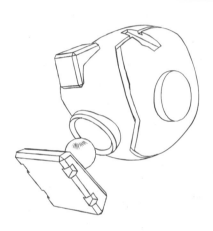

Pleated Type
Even though this kind of neck is easy to move around and looks smart, it generates a silly atmosphere and is not generally used for hero robots.

The tubes and cords wrapped around the neck give reality to the robots. This is especially so for scenes when the robots are getting repaired or being destroyed. Drawing pressurized air or oil makes the scenes even more realistic.

Different Ways to Draw the Head with Perspective

It originally had been a helmet-shaped head, however, with additional decorations, it now looks very heroic.

By adding an additional part that looks like hair, a simple design like this can become very feminine.

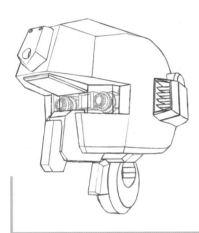

This design, with cameras inside the eyes, is often used for realistically looking robots.

By drawing each part larger than usual, the head looks very stable and balanced.

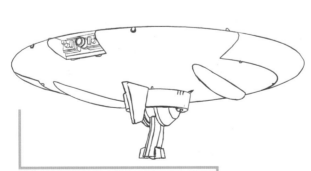

A disk-shaped head. It resembles radars for airplanes.

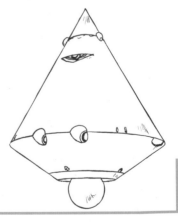

By using geometric shapes and placing the eyes in an unusual spot, the face now seems very mysterious.

The gas mask makes the face cold and expressionless.

Using animalistic shapes can give a devilish impression.

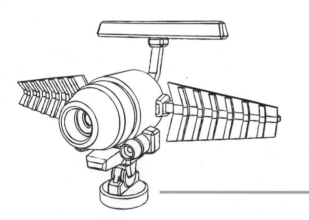

A combination of radar and camera makes this design look more machine-like than the disk-shaped design.

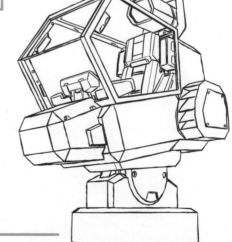

The cockpit design. It is the best design for a viewer to figure out its size.

Samples of Frames Using the Head

The viewpoint can change the expression or the feeling of the robot. Visors and ledges can be used to express different feelings. Same as the acting style of Japanese No, you can express feelings without using facial expressions.

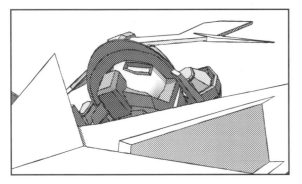

The upward angle makes the robot seem dependable and trustworthy.

It is possible to make it feel like someone or something is approaching the robot from behind by making the robot face backward - away from the viewpoint.

A crane shot focusing downward on the robot with only an eye gazing back make the robot seem angry and that it is staring.

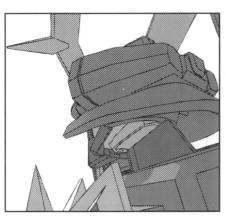

Focusing lines and the sound effects make it seem like the robot's eyes are focusing on something.

A counter-light with the focus on the eyes brings out the robot's intelligence.

CHAPTER 3
The Body

The body can be divided into three parts: the chest, the stomach and the hip. However, the stomach may be edited off the design from time to time.
In this chapter, we will mainly talk about parts for the chest and the hip.

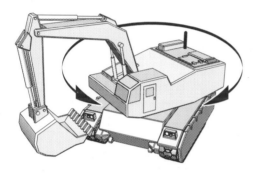

Some robots have cockpits, engines, fuel tanks, or weapons inside their body, but it is important that the body must stay flexible and ready to move. This is so especially for human-shaped robots because they need to act and move like humans.

It is very difficult to express any human-like qualities of a robot if it had a body like this power shovel, which can only rotate left or right. (However, it is possible to use this design for machine-like robots.)

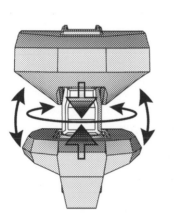

It is ideal for a robot body to be able to move freely in any direction possible. As seen in the illustration, the stomach part needs to be small in order to avoid bothering the movement of the other two parts. Also, this design is suited for showing masculinity of a well-trained body. However, there are some exceptions…

There are some robots without the body but with their backbones directly attached to the head. This kind of minimum, fundamental design tells that robots were designed to resemble human bodies, and also that the body part is a variation of the backbone.

Because it has become very popular to design the joints flexible and movable, the body is an essential part containing many joints.

Basic for Drawing the Body with Perspective

The body is usually situated in the center and it is where most of its tools and gears are placed. When drawing the body, you should divide it into three parts: 1) around the neck, 2) around the stomach and 3) around the hip. Also, keep in mind how you will connect the limbs to the body, what kind of function the robot will have, and the overall image when drawing out the rough sketch. We will talk about the stomach and the hip areas together.

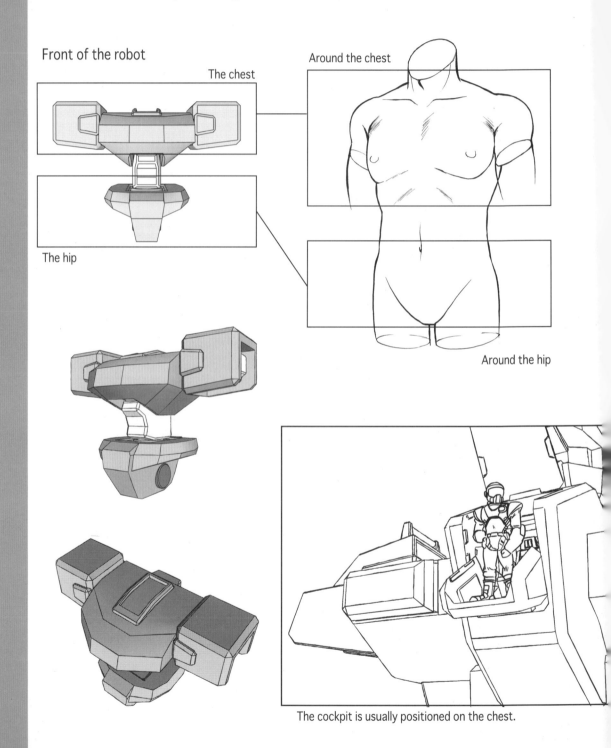

Front of the robot

The chest

The hip

Around the chest

Around the hip

The cockpit is usually positioned on the chest.

The Balance of the Body

Stretched/shrunk vertically (slow/fast)
Stretched/shrunk horizontally (weapon placed inside/suited for fighting)

Stretched/shrunk vertically

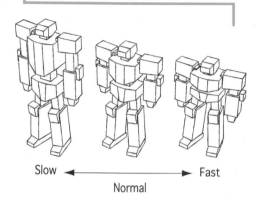

Slow ←——————→ Fast
Normal

Stretched/shrunk horizontally

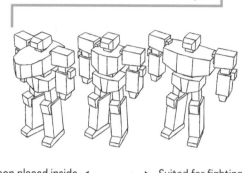

Weapon placed inside ←——————→ Suited for fighting
Normal

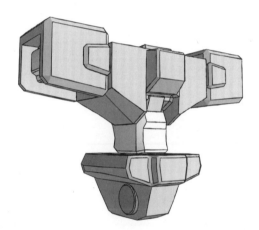

Because it is quite common to attach extra parts on the body, it might be a good idea to draw a few extra joints.

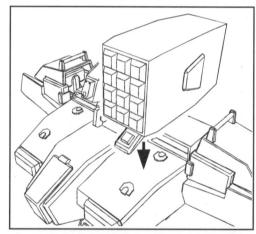

Although the back of a robot is often neglected, it sometimes appears on scenes when the robots are being repaired. Design it carefully.

It usually has hatches and ducts, thus it is not so common to have decorations or weapons attached.

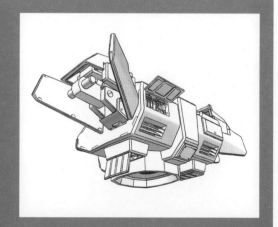

Different Ways to Draw the Chest (Straight lines)

The chest is fairly easy to design nicely and machine-like. You can also give softness to the designs by adjusting the angles. However, it can turn out to be time-consuming.

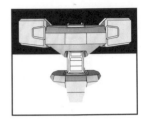

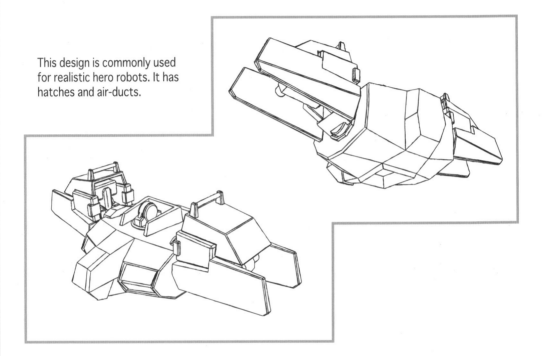

This design is commonly used for realistic hero robots. It has hatches and air-ducts.

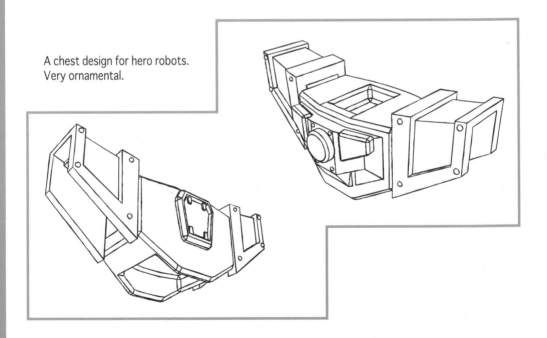

A chest design for hero robots. Very ornamental.

A design for realistic and serious robots. They Contains a lot of details on censor-related tools.

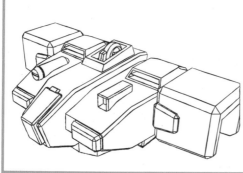

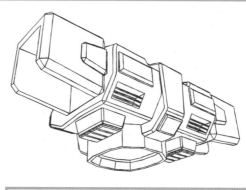

A design for machine-like robots. There is a camera placed in the opening in the center. Arms will be attached to the shoulder parts.

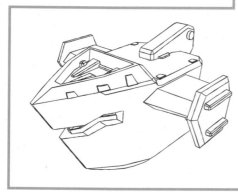

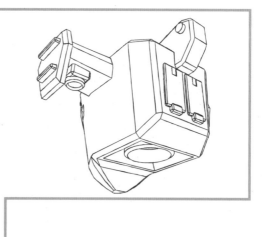

A design for realistic female robots. Although it contains many straight lines, their angles bring out femininity.

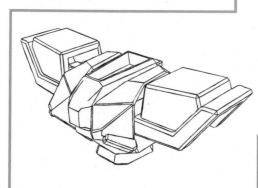

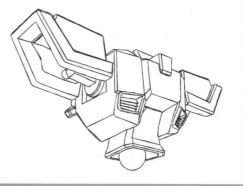

Different Ways to Draw the Chest (Curved lines)

This design is suited to express strength; it also has lively feeling. However, robots with round shape designs can seem like they were made by machines. It's possible to design these round-shaped chests with very few lines, but it could become very difficult to maintain the balance.

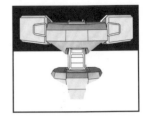

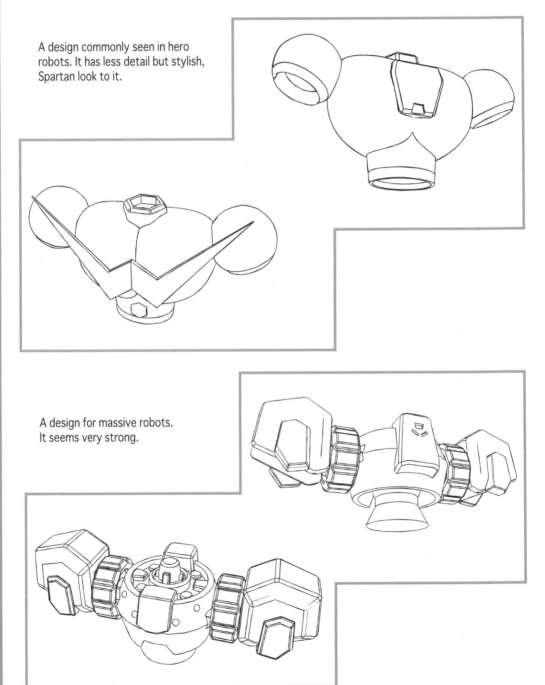

A design commonly seen in hero robots. It has less detail but stylish, Spartan look to it.

A design for massive robots. It seems very strong.

A simple cylindrical design. Cute.

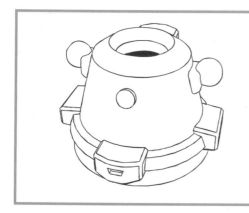
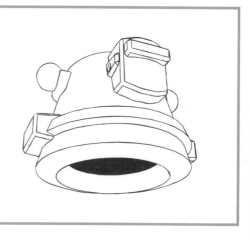

This is designed to look like it was made from a waste. An additional head on the chest makes it unique.

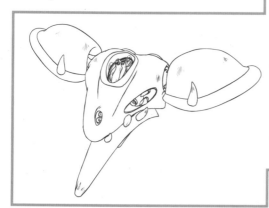
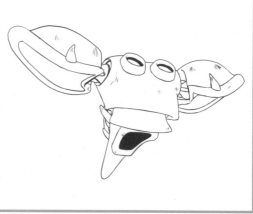

A simple design for female robots. Very feminine.

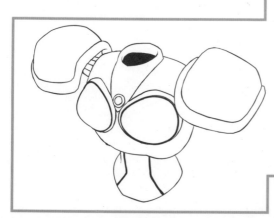
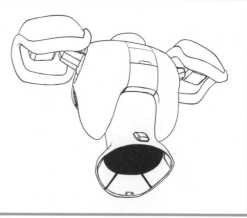

Different Ways to Draw the Hip

The hip usually needs to be compatible with the chest and the legs. When you take off the outer cover, you will see that the hip is made of many joints.

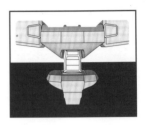

T-shaped Type

This design is very common in plastic models. The name "T" comes from the shape of a piece that is beneath all the armor. This designs and the design without the bulge on the top, which are quite popular were created from the shorts type.

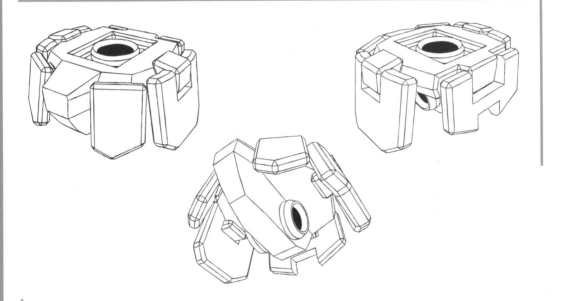

Shorts Type

A very simple design with Spartan look. Commonly seen in old-fashioned robots.

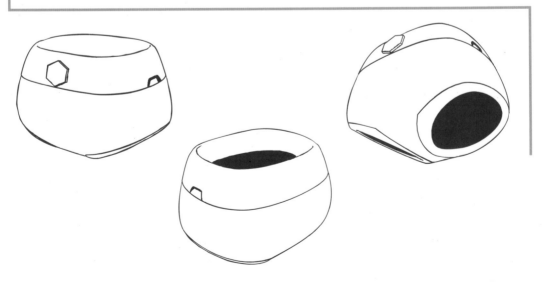

Swinging Leg Type

Often used for enemy robots. It is easy to add legs because it has no crotch. Because of its mobility, this design is used in real life robots. However, it is not a common design for animation/manga robots.

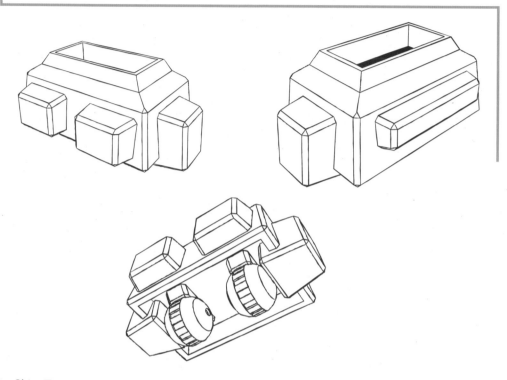

Skirt Type

It is called a skirt type because of the shape of its stretched armor around the hip. This design is fairly common because of the easiness to add thruster and gimmicks.

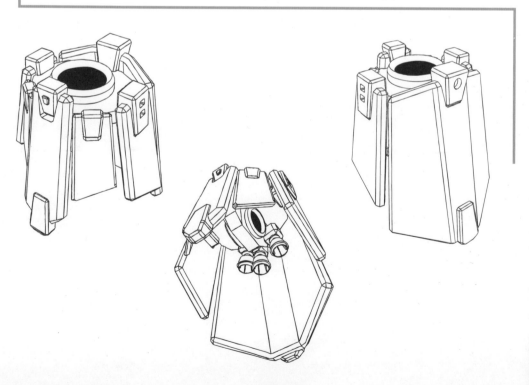

Optional Equipments for the Back /How to Attach Them

Cannon Type [Attachable with a bolt]
Once attached it cannot be taken off by the robot itself.
A scene with the robot being equipped with this piece can be very impressive.

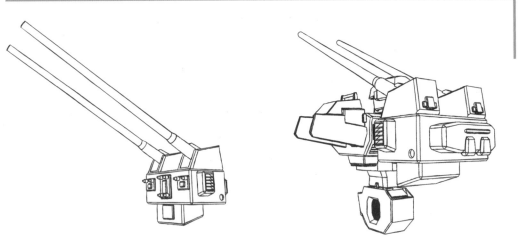

Missile Container Type [Attachable with a hook]
It is detachable after finishing using it. Can be used in a scene where ally robots are attaching this kind of equipment on each other's backs.

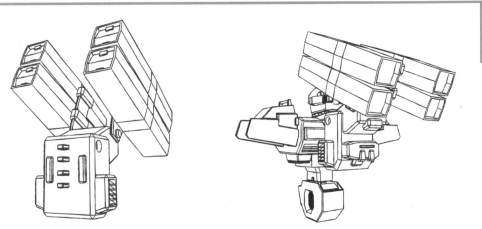

Flying Device Type [Attachable with a belt]
The way to attach this equipment can vary depending on the design of the robot - it may not be necessary to use any attachment device.

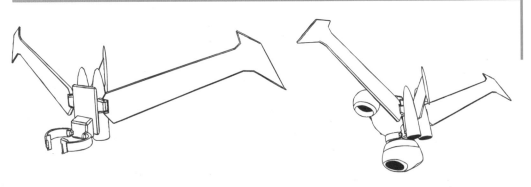

Tank Type [Attachable with magnets]

An easy design with simple lines. However, it might be better to come up with additional attachment devices for more stability.

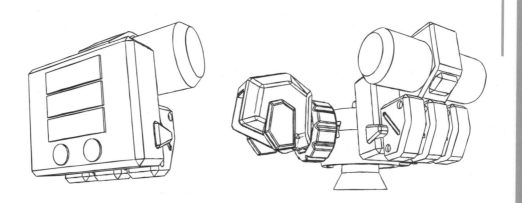

Container Type [Worn as a backpack]

It is very easy to attach this type - simply worn on the robot's back. However, it lacks balance and solidness. Good for life-size robots.

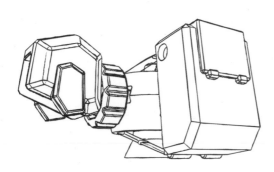

Screw Unit Type [Attachable with suckers]

It is a simple design that goes nicely with robots with smooth surface. Cannot be used in outer space.

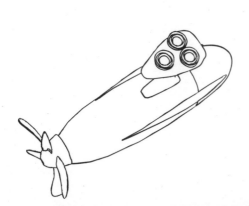
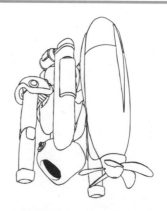

There are many more optional equipments and ways to attach them.

Different Ways to Draw the Body with Perspectives

A winged design suitable for hero robots. It is more ornamental than being practical.

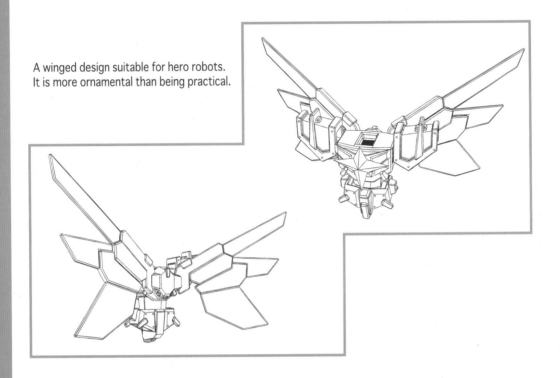

A design with cannons for realistic/serious robots. Simple.

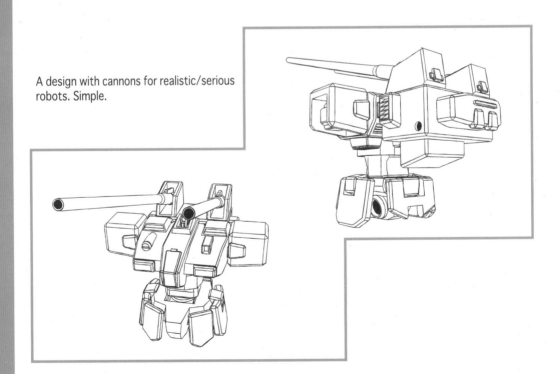

A design for massive robots.
It has more width than length.

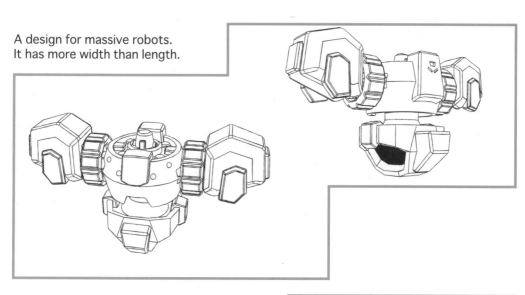

A design with a skirt type hip attached.
Suited for realistic female robots. Very elegant.

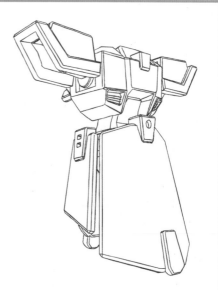

A design with a shorts type hip attached.
Commonly used for simple female robots.
Very athletic.

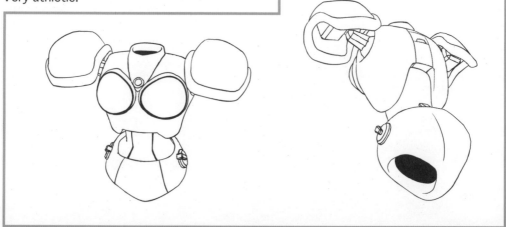

Samples of Frames Using the Body

Pull out a huge weapon.

Create an image of strength and sturdiness.

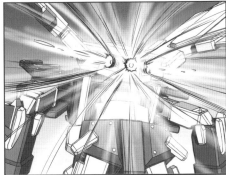

The use of an upward angle creates immensity.

CHAPTER 4
The Arms

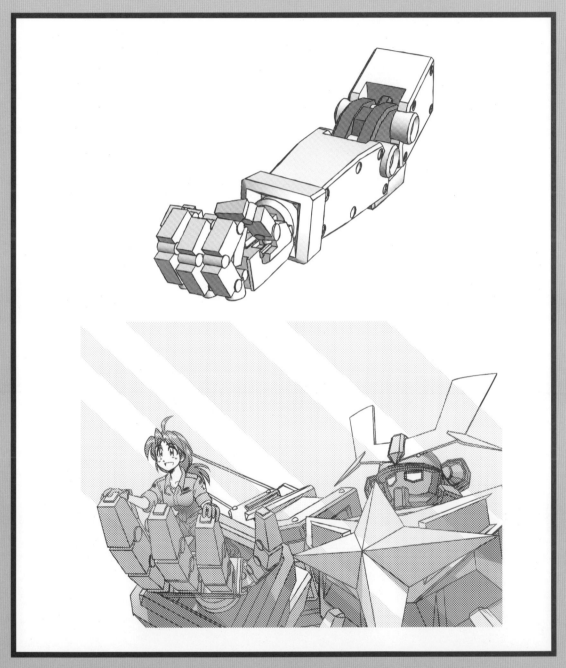

When drawing the arms, you should pay extra attention to the shoulder joints, the elbows and their joints, and the hands. The patterns can change dramatically just by adding weapons.

Basics for Drawing the Arms

Basic Perspective

When drawing the arms, you should pay extra attention to the shoulder joints, the elbows and their joints, and the hands.

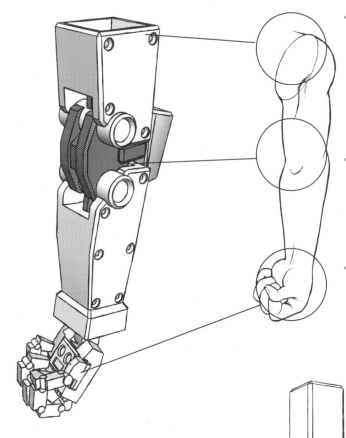

Shoulder
In a robot's body, this part is inside the shoulder covers and usually connects the arms to the body. A complicated design of this section can prove to be difficult because of its frequent use.

Elbow
Made of one or two joints. Easy to add small details.

Hand
An essential part for tool-using robots. It can be replaced with or attached to a weapon. This part is easy to create many different patterns.

By placing the joint inside, the mobility expands even with only one joint.

Double-jointed Type

By doubling the joint, it expands the hand's mobility. The idea was taken from the joints of a plastic model.

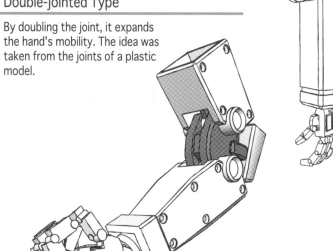

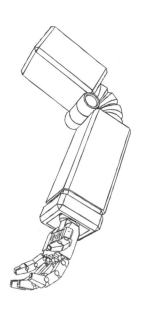

Balancing the Arms

Although drawing long arms is fairly common, short arms are never used for robot designs. This is probably due to the fact that short arms look incapable of holding any object. However, it might be possible to use them to express a sense of inconvenience. Arms designed too long or too short are sometimes seen in times of metamorphosis or two robots combining together, however, they may spoil the human-like feeling of the robot(s).

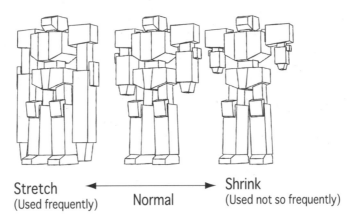

Stretch
(Used frequently)
← Normal →
Shrink
(Used not so frequently)

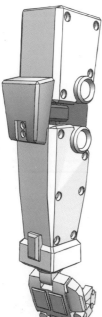

Details of the Arms

Arms with too much detail can become very confusing at times. The joints and the palms usually have the most detail; try to keep the overall design simple to maintain the balance.

Elbow Protector

Although it can be excluded, it adds spice to the picture.

All the details are focused on the inside of the joints.

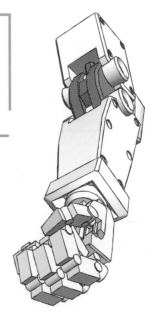

Most joints are on the palms. Many lines are needed.

Censors on the fingertips make the hands look very machine-like.

Different Ways to Draw the Elbow Joints/Human-shaped Arms

Hero Robot Type

A simple, double-jointed design with few lines. The elbow protector serves as a blade-shaped weapon.

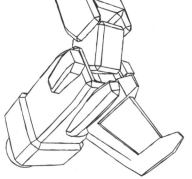
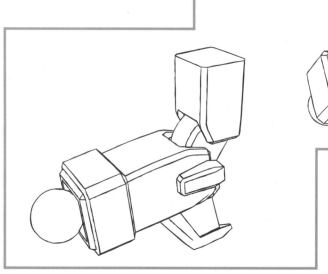

Realistic Robot Type

It is fairly common for realistic robots to have many small details. This is due to the fact that they are fully equipped with many tools and equipments. They are sometimes equipped with movable elbow protectors with shields.

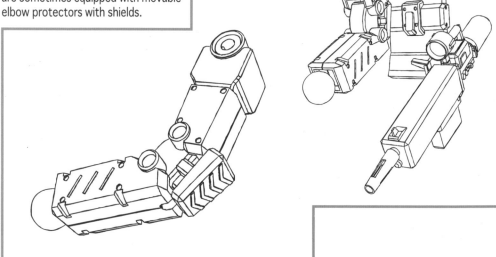

Massive Robot Type
A simple design, but the cylindrical shape gives strength. By using pleated joint, the arm seems like it can move freely in any direction.

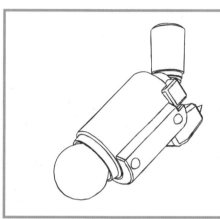
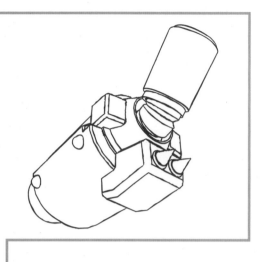

Multi-jointed Type
It is usually used for labor robots but sometimes can be used for monster robots. This kind of design looks more like an industrial machine manipulator than an arm for a robot. Possible to attach a sub-arm.

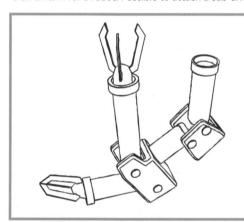
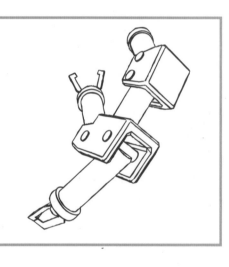

Pleated Type
It is very flexible without any joints.
It can be used as a tentacle.

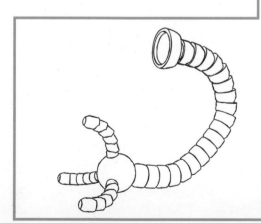
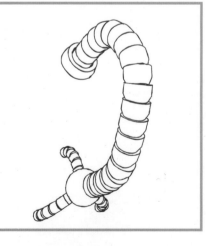

Different Ways to Draw the Hands/Palms

Human-shaped

The most common design. The hands seem capable of functioning as those of human's.

Five fingered/Square Type

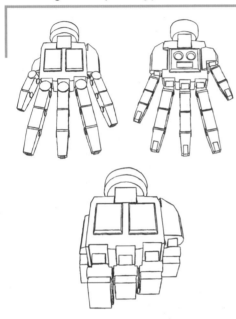

Five fingered/Round Type

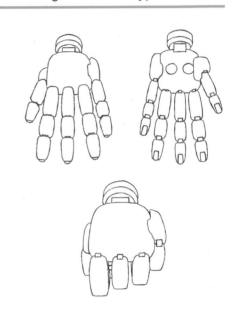

Three fingered Type
This design looks strong but low at cost.

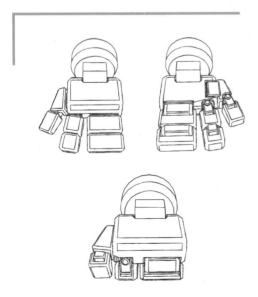

Five fingered/Hooked nails Type
These sharpened fingers (nails) can be used as weapons, also.

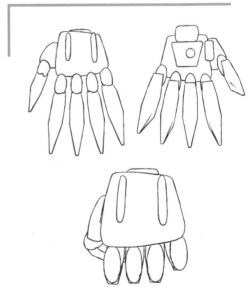

Manipulator-shaped Designs

Manipulator is a kind of fake mechanical hands attached to machines - usually to space shuttles and deep-sea submarines. It functions as cutting pliers or tongues.

Four fingered/Square Type
Suited for labor robots.

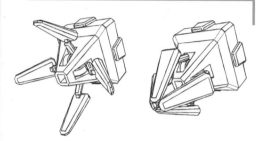

Three fingered/Round Type
Suited for labor robots.

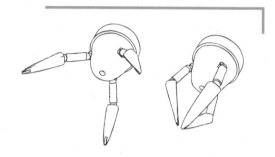

Clamp Type

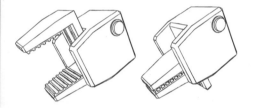

Magnetic Type
Suckers can be used, also.

Special Models

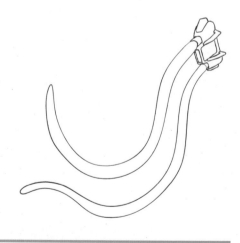

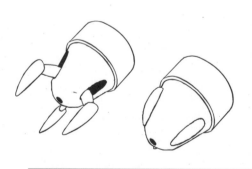

Nail-shaped Type
Becomes a hammer when folded.

Tentacle Type
Very flexible and can be used as a whip.

Different Ways to Draw Nonhuman-like Arms

These very machine-like parts are designed to replace the arms.

Drill Type
As you can see, this type can be used to drill out holes. It is better, though, to have the attachments changeable because using the same weapon over and over again can get very dull.

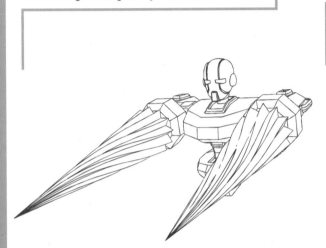

Stake Type
This type can also make holes, however, by stinging the enemy.

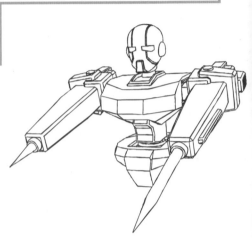

Extendable Arm Type
The arms can be extended (or shortened) to grab something or punch someone far away.

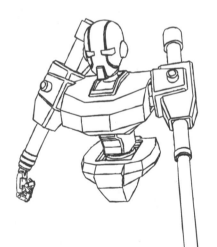

Tentacle Type
This type can be used to grab objects or used as a whip.

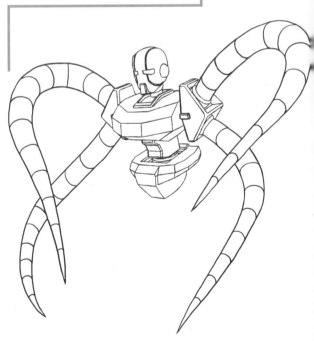

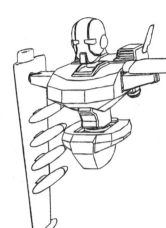

Wing Type
For airborne battles.
This type is not suited for battles on land.

Cannon Type
Designed for artillery attacks. This type is very destructive, but not suited for close battles because of its heavy weight.

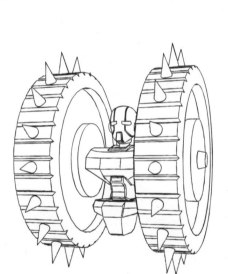

Spiked Wheel Type
This type can be used to roll and attack the enemy directly. However, the wheels need to be carefully designed so they wouldn't block out the sight.

Missile Type
It cannot hold many missiles, but the robot can detach the containers after using up all the missiles.

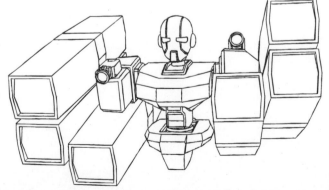

Different Ways to Draw Handheld Weapons

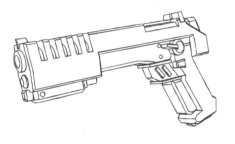

Pistol
Pistols for huge robots differ from those for humans. Most of them are controlled by switches inside the cockpit. When the switch is pressed, the trigger transmits the signal and then fires a bullet. (However there are some that function like the usual type)

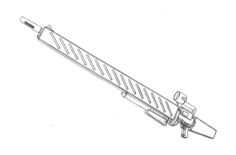

Rifle
Being generally strong, most robots carry these rifles rather than the pistols. The shoulder stocks can be ornamental at times, although some robots don't have them entirely.

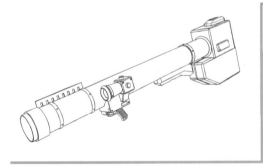

Bazooka
A very popular weapon for robots. It can be transformed to a missile launcher.

Missile Pod
Suitable for small robots because large robots usually have this installed inside them.

Gattling gun
It is becoming a popular weapon for robots. A scene using this weapon with empty cartridges falling down can be very impressive.

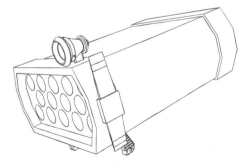
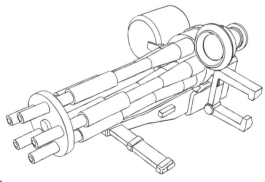

Sword/Shield/Spear

These medieval weapons enlarged for being used by robots are frequently used by hero robots due to their good looks.

Hatchet with Boosters / Machete with Beam-guns

Additional devices make these normal weapons sufficient for robot use. An example of ancient and latest technologies combined.

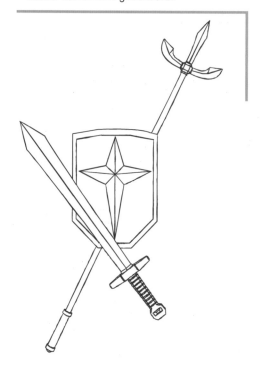

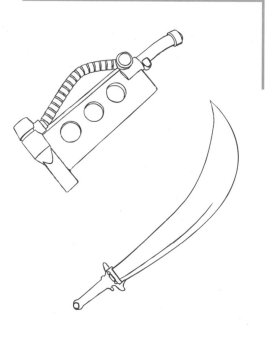

Shield

A realistic shield. The device within the shield relaxes the shock of any bullets hitting it.

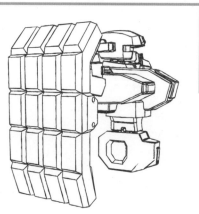

Huge Hammer with Boosters

Impossible to be used by humans, this gigantic hammer is easily handled by robots. The boosters add speed.

Different Ways to Draw the Arms with Perspectives

Hero Robot Type
The emphasis is on the silhouette. Very impressive but with few lines.

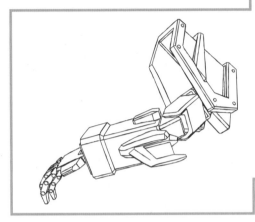
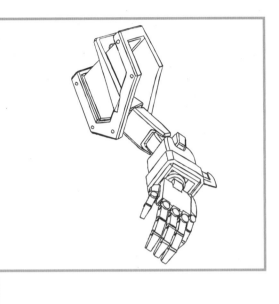

Massive Robot Type
The emphasis is on the outline; strong and impressive.

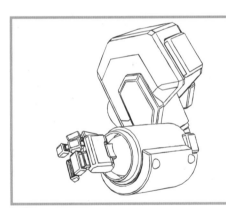
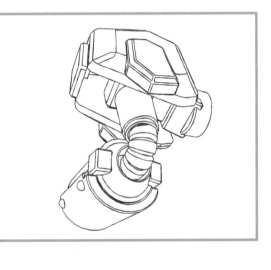

Realistic Robot Type
Delicate lines give a machine-like look.

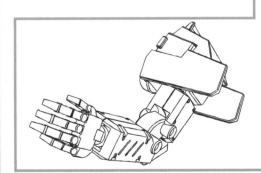
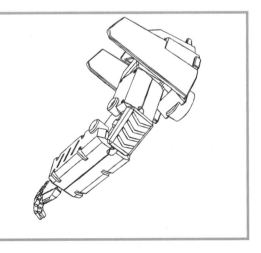

Female Robot Type
Curved lines bring out softness.

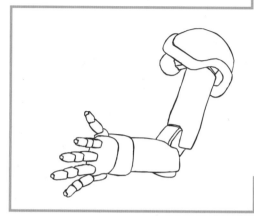
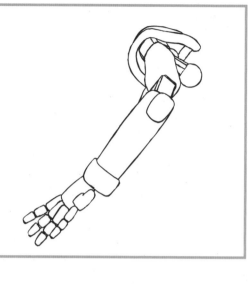

Monster Robot Type
Nonhuman-like features.

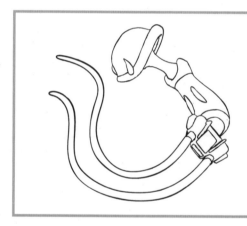

Multi-jointed Robot Type
Machine-like feeling.

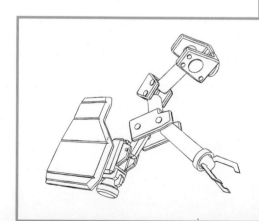
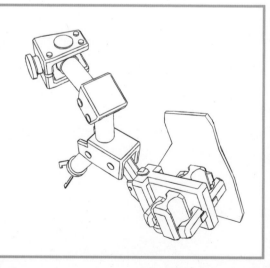

Samples of Frames Using the Arms

Grab

Punch
Try to use the perspective effectively.

An object on the robot's hand gives a sense of immensity to the robot.

CHAPTER 5
The Legs

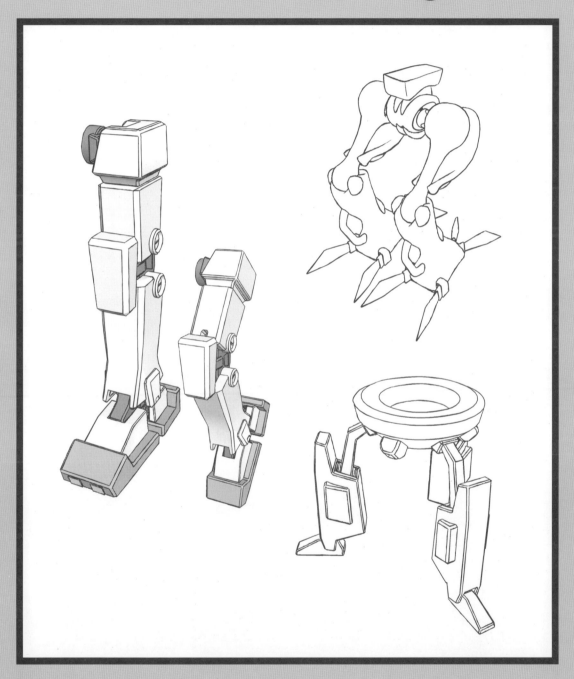

The three important areas of the legs are the joint of the hip, the knee, and the ankle. Unlike the hands, they need balance since they support the whole body.

Basics for Drawing the Legs

The same with the sample of the hands, this sample is double-jointed.

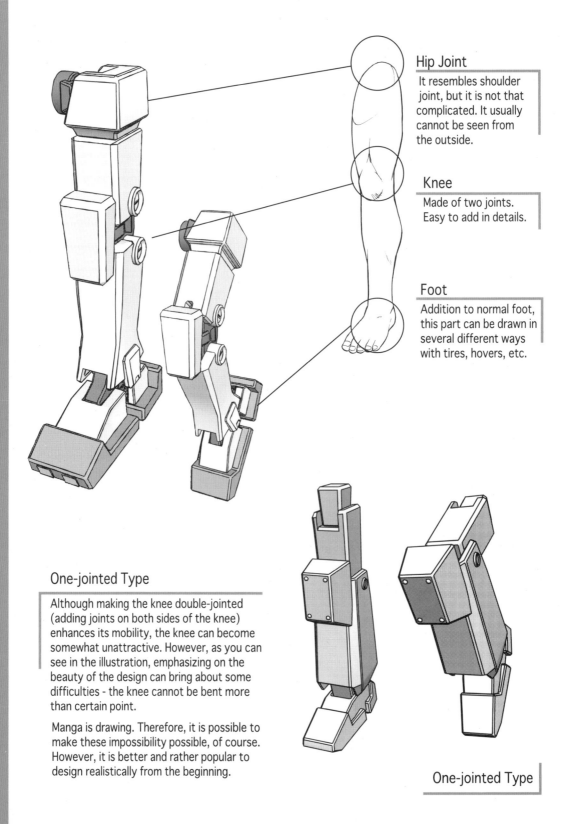

Hip Joint
It resembles shoulder joint, but it is not that complicated. It usually cannot be seen from the outside.

Knee
Made of two joints. Easy to add in details.

Foot
Addition to normal foot, this part can be drawn in several different ways with tires, hovers, etc.

One-jointed Type
Although making the knee double-jointed (adding joints on both sides of the knee) enhances its mobility, the knee can become somewhat unattractive. However, as you can see in the illustration, emphasizing on the beauty of the design can bring about some difficulties - the knee cannot be bent more than certain point.

Manga is drawing. Therefore, it is possible to make these impossibility possible, of course. However, it is better and rather popular to design realistically from the beginning.

One-jointed Type

Balancing the Length of the Legs
The length and the thickness changes the impression.

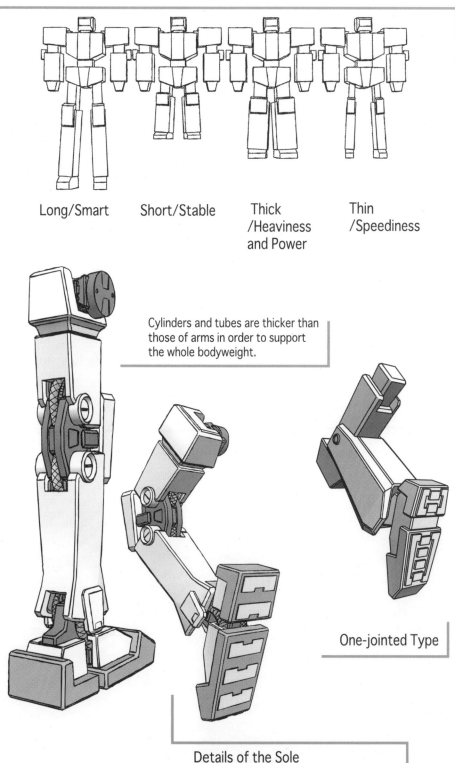

Long/Smart   Short/Stable   Thick /Heaviness and Power   Thin /Speediness

Cylinders and tubes are thicker than those of arms in order to support the whole bodyweight.

One-jointed Type

Details of the Sole
Parts or clasps to avoid slipping, and air ducts can be added.

Different Ways to Draw Human-shaped Legs and Knees

Hero Robot Type

A relatively simple silhouette with decorations on the knee.
A common design.

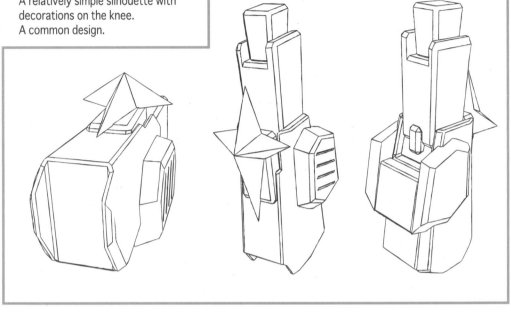

Realistic Robot Type

It is a delicate design with many lines with a device added to avoid slipping.
A standard design.

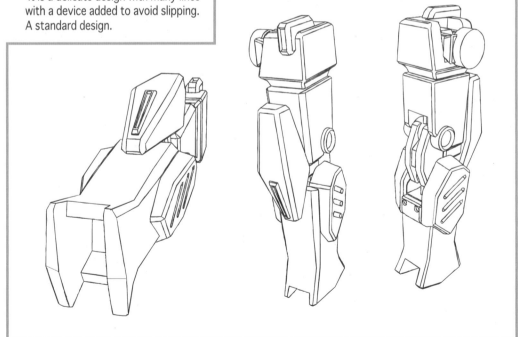

Massive Robot Type

A solid silhouette with a heat radiator duct. A heavyweight image.

Female Robot Type

This type has a slender silhouette. Smaller knees create a light image.

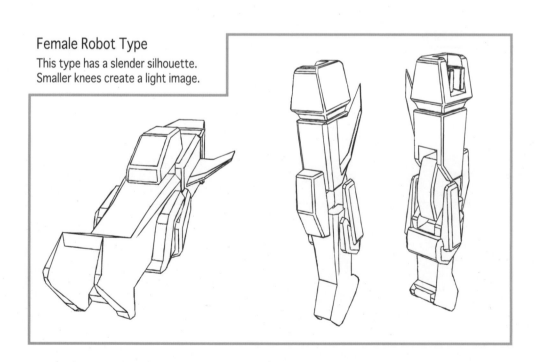

Different Ways to Draw Nonhuman-like Legs

Monster Robot Type
The reversed joints of the knees and the hooked nails create a grotesque image.

Three-legged Robot Type
Although well-balanced, having three legs unlike any living matter makes this design eccentric.

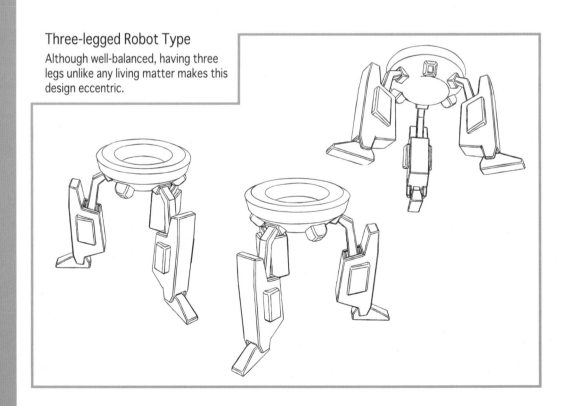

Four-legged Robot Type

The tail can be replaced by a weapon. Very well-balanced and any kind of animal can be adapted to this design.

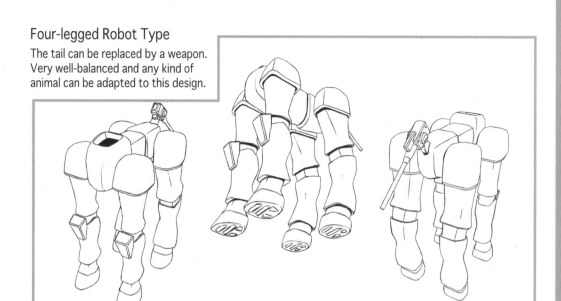

Multi-legged Robot Type

Although it has balance, this design, which resembles the legs of an insect or a crustacean has an alien feeling to it.

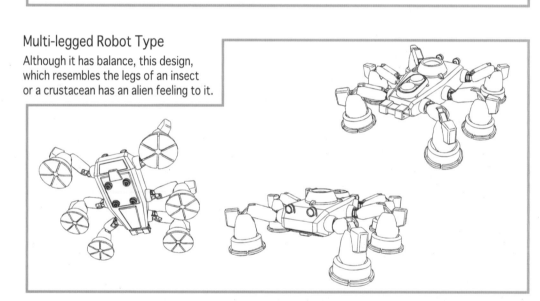

Tank Type

The tank can replace the body of a robot.

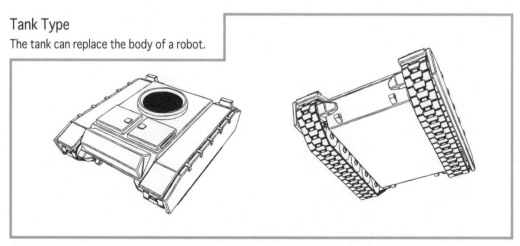

Different Ways to Draw Parts Below the Ankles

Normal Grip Type
A standard and simple design.

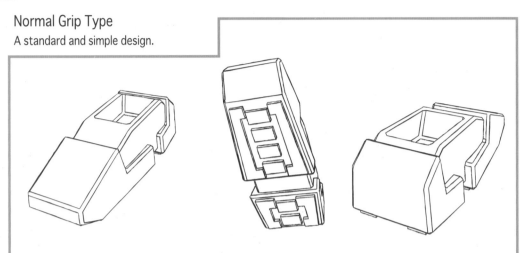

Normal Grip + Veneer Type
With the veneer, it is suitable for outer space.

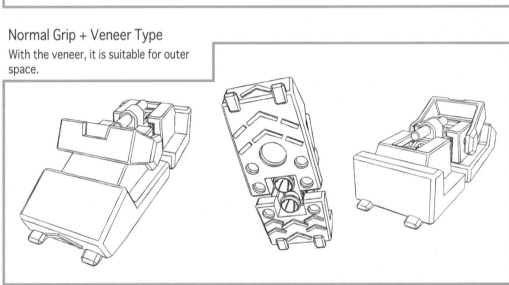

Tire Type
The tires enable the robot to run at high speed. However, when the robot cannot use the tires, it can walk normally.

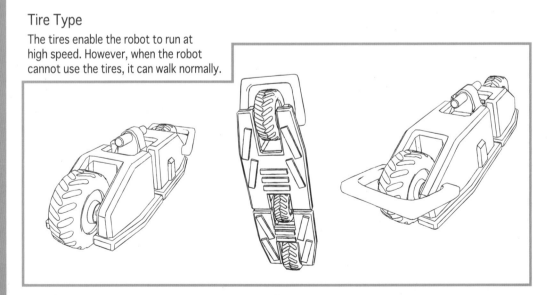

Dynamic + Veneer
Old-fashioned and very simple.

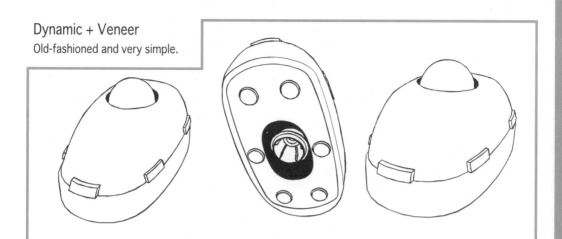

Hover Type
This type can be used on water, but not really suited for delicate moves.

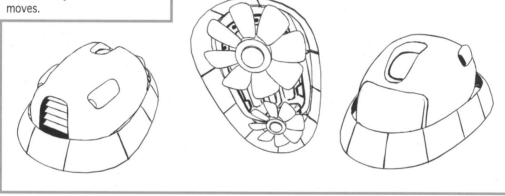

Hooked Nails Type
This type can be used as a weapon also. It can be used to grab something as well.

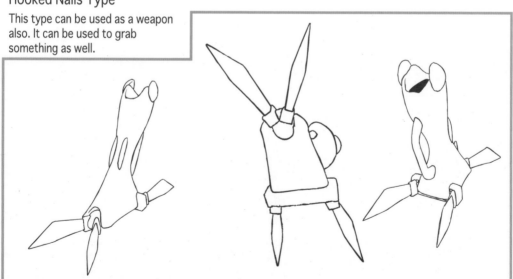

Different Ways to Draw the Legs with Perspectives

Hero Robot Type

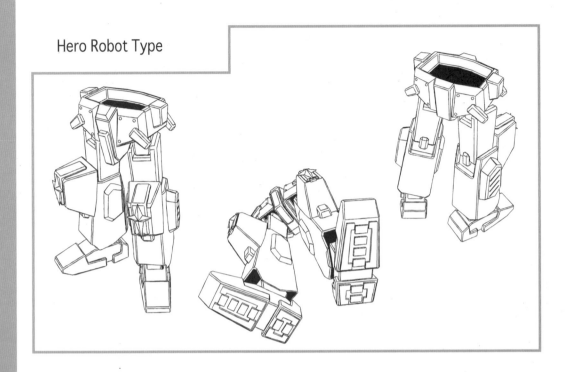

Realistic Robot Type

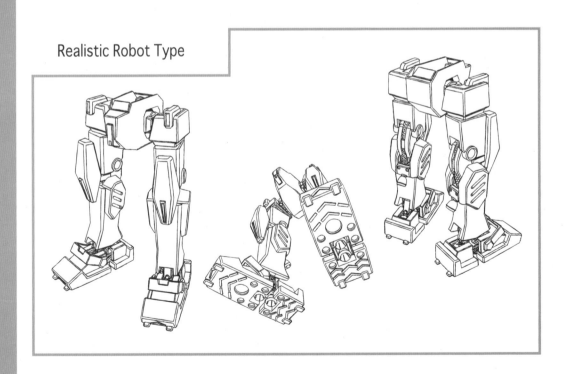

Massive Robot Type

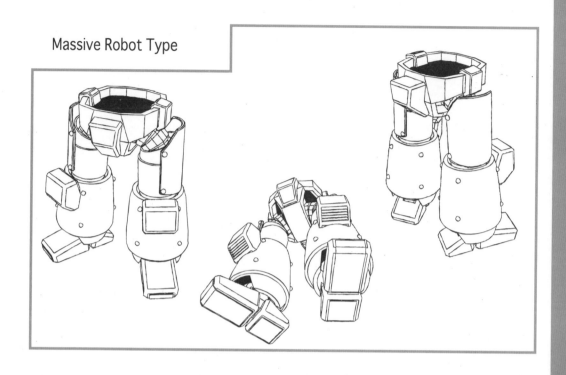

Female Robot Type

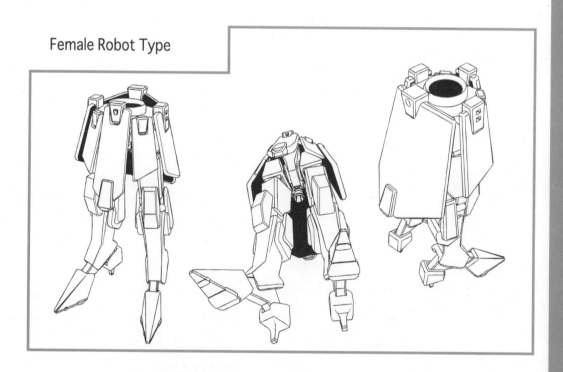

Samples of Frames Using the Legs

Stomping (crushing)
Sound effects and smoke can add reality to a scene of a robot running a dash.

Kick
By adding details like flying robot parts and effect lines can effectively show the robot's powerfulness.

Roller Dash
The heaviness of the robot which comes from the angle and the rockets add reality.

No Gravity
Be careful of the balance of the limbs and the angle.

CHAPTER 6
Variety of Robot Design

It is possible to create a variety of robot designs just by adding/changing small details like optional parts and decorations.

Variety of Robot Design

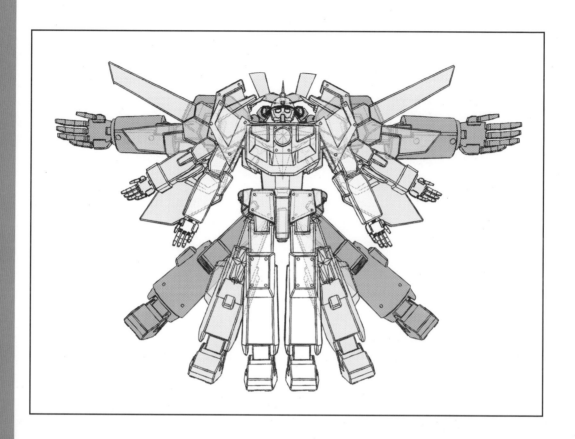

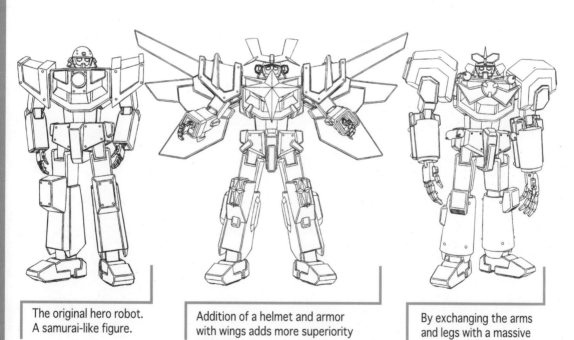

The original hero robot. A samurai-like figure.

Addition of a helmet and armor with wings adds more superiority and power. It now looks like a samurai general.

By exchanging the arms and legs with a massive robot, it now looks like a Buddhist monk warrior.

Hero Mechanical Robot (Slender Type)

A rectangular design. Broad chest and shoulders with slender limbs give a speedy impression to the robot. It looks very heroic with swords and spears.

The pose with the sword in hand addition to the wings and the helmet brings out the fierceness of the robot.

The sound effect and the words written according to the perspective make this scene very realistic and unique.

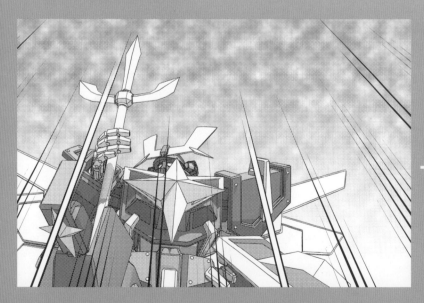

A dynamic scene of the robot taking out its weapon from its body.

Massive Robot

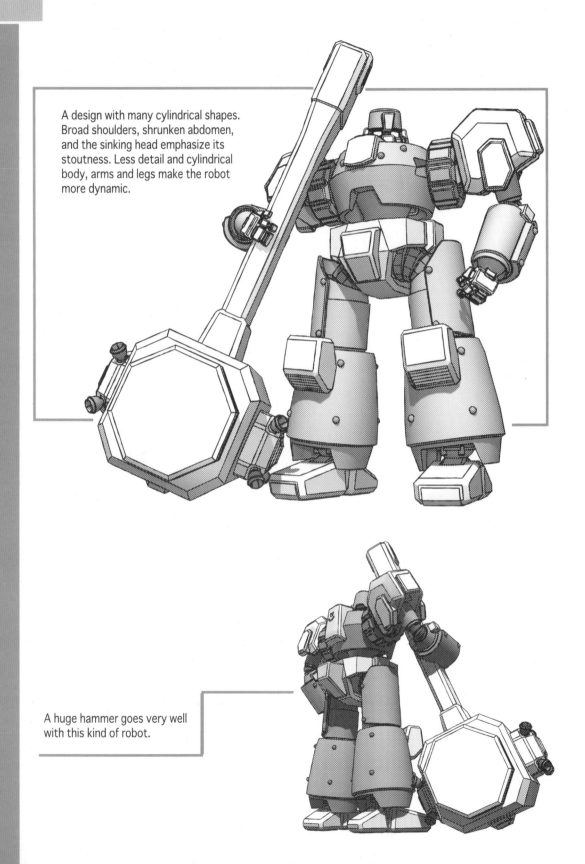

A design with many cylindrical shapes. Broad shoulders, shrunken abdomen, and the sinking head emphasize its stoutness. Less detail and cylindrical body, arms and legs make the robot more dynamic.

A huge hammer goes very well with this kind of robot.

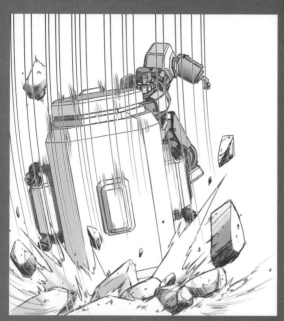
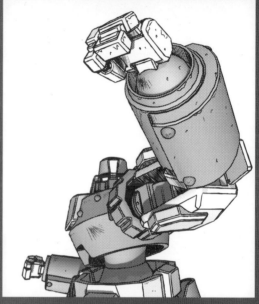
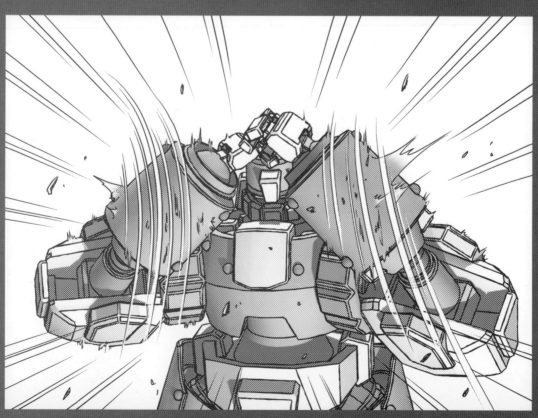

Monster Robot

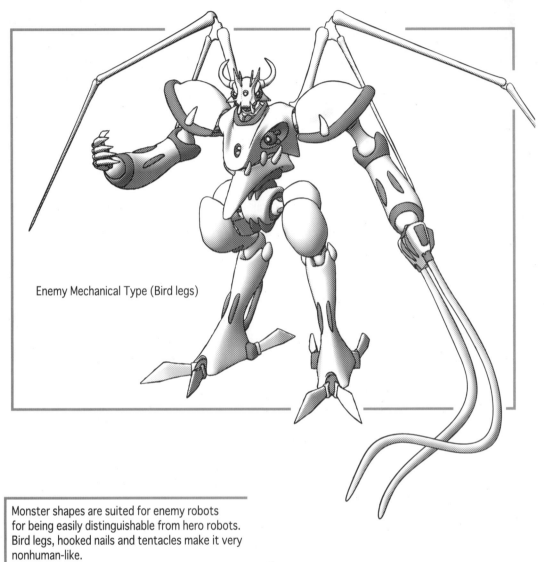

Enemy Mechanical Type (Bird legs)

Monster shapes are suited for enemy robots for being easily distinguishable from hero robots. Bird legs, hooked nails and tentacles make it very nonhuman-like.

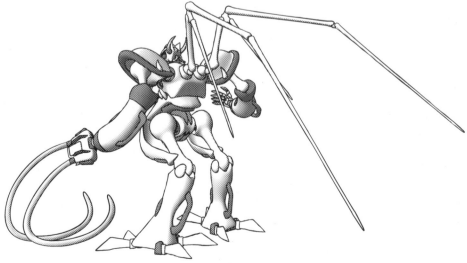

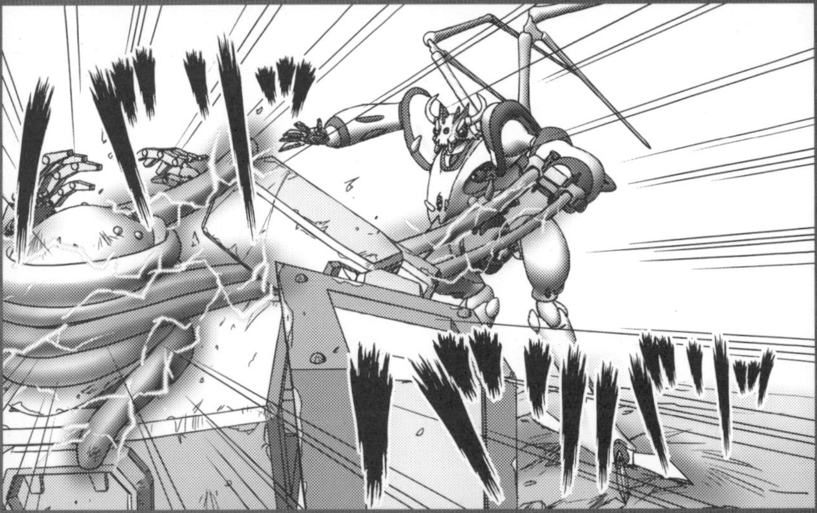
バリッ
バリバリッ

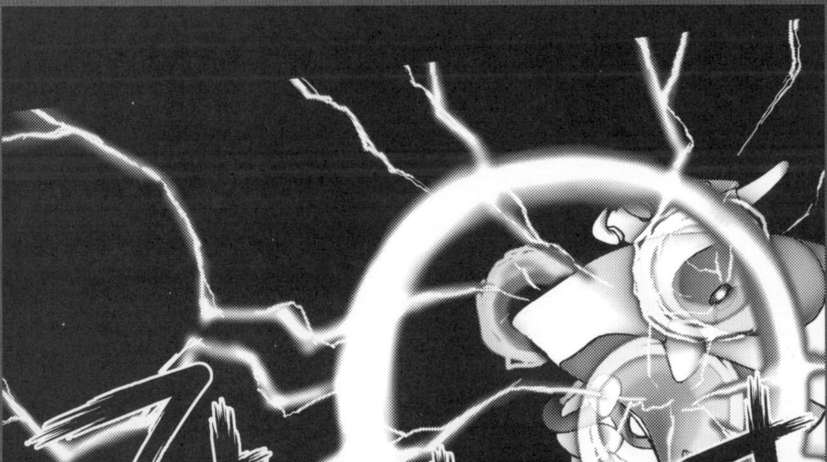
フォオオオオ

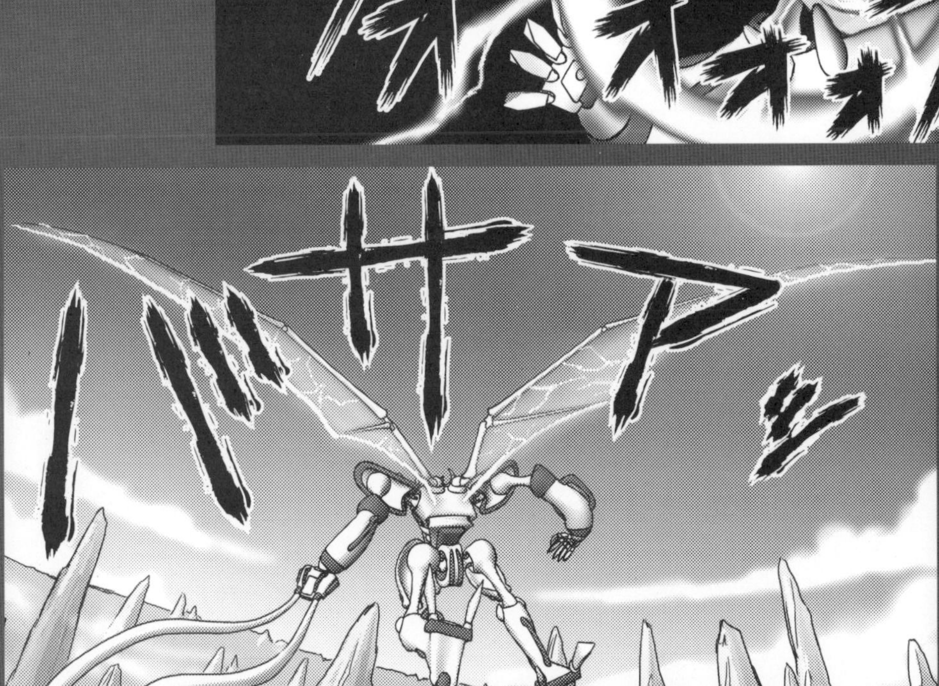
バサァ

Female Robot (Adult)

It is better to use pentagons or hexagons to emphasize the female robot's softness while using straight lines. The chest area, hair attachment, and the high-heels-inspired footing make this design unique. The robot's chest is installed with missiles, and the boomerang makes it very dynamic.

BUN
FOOM!

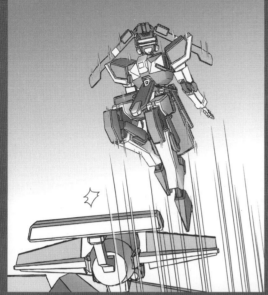

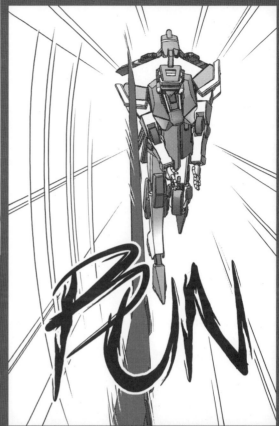

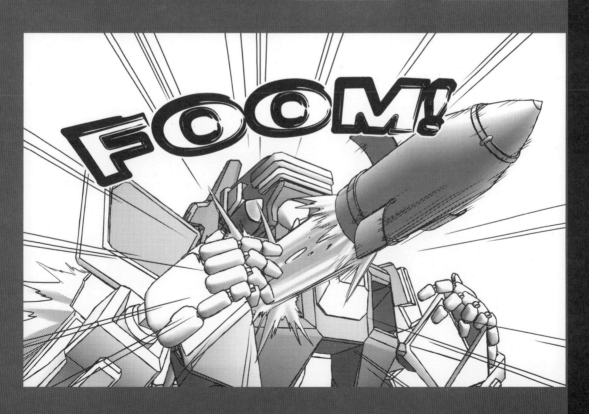

Female Robot (Young)

It is ideal not to emphasize the robot's bodyline. The ribbon on the chest, pigtails, and the large round eyes make the robot very cute. This kind of robot is not suitable for combats, thus its size is small. This type of robot can easily be used in scenes where the robot interacts with humans or animals. Changing the optional parts can change the impression of the robot.

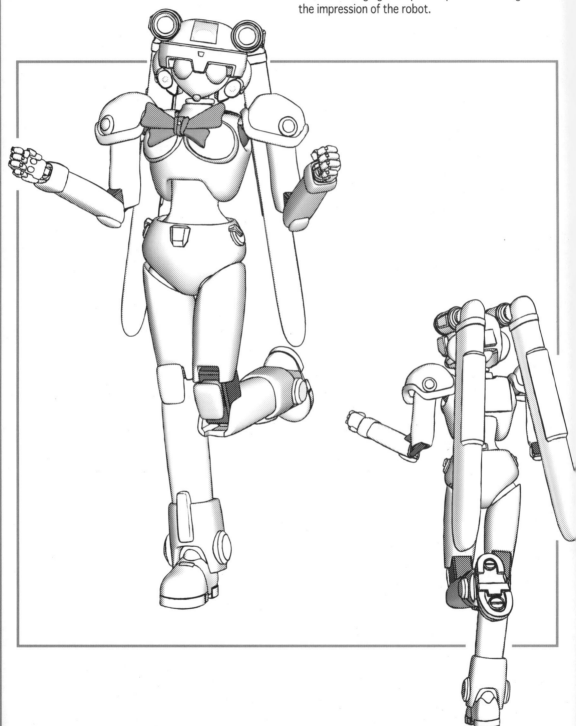

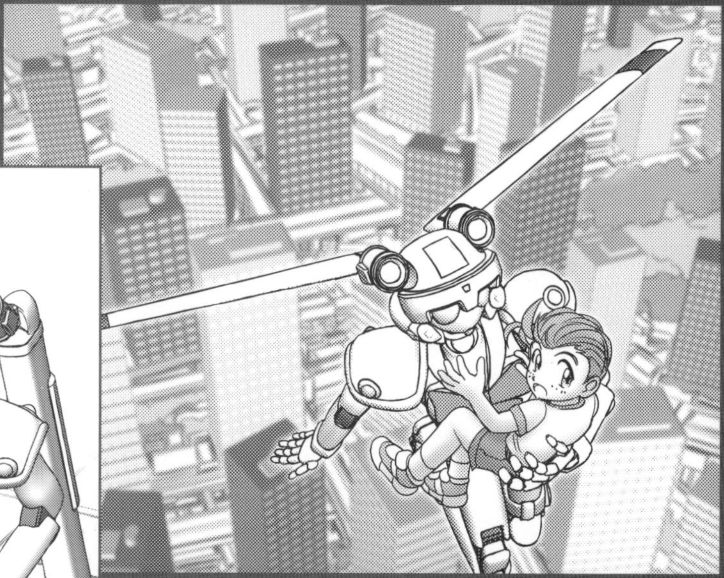

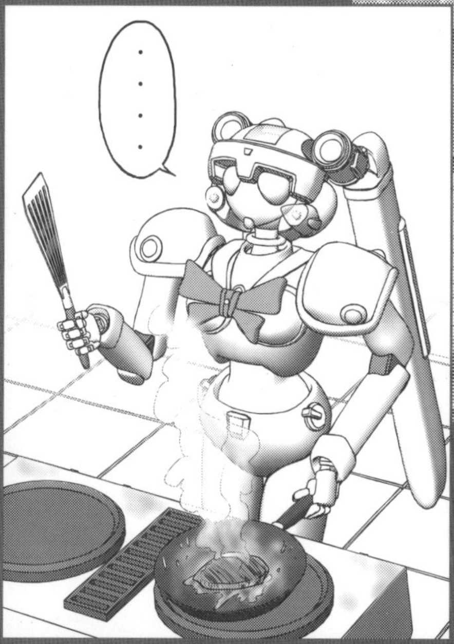

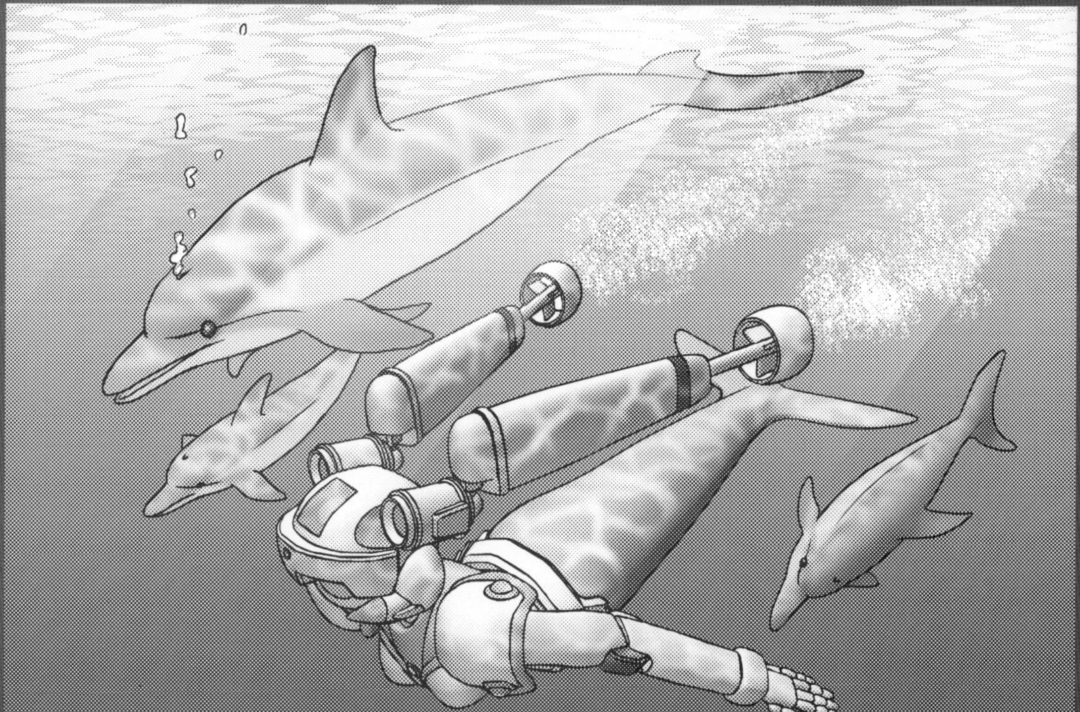

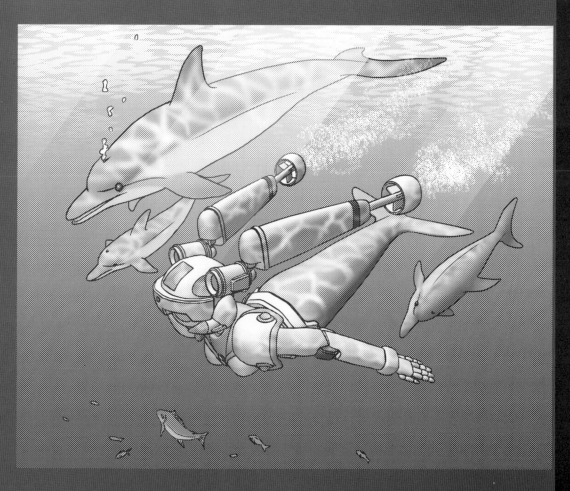

Multi-legged Robot

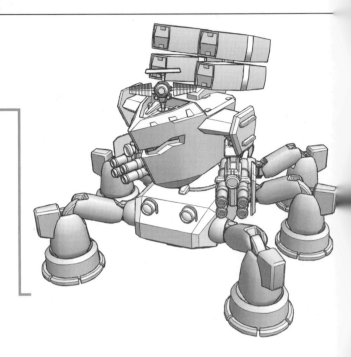

The legs, of course, are its chief feature. The sample resembles a scorpion. Unlike human-shaped robots, it gives a very bizarre impression. This has missile launchers on its upper part of the body, creating a tank-like look, but these can be replaced by upper part of a human-shaped body.

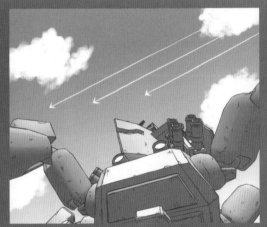